THE
RAVER STORIES
PROJECT

To Sean (Sean Young)
Guess What?
You are Mentioned in
My Story in chapter 17. Enjoy?!
Five Love, Dance
Besitos and all the Best
You fan

Margaret Helen Schlamp

— MARGARET Schlamp

ALSO from **5150 Publishing**

DANCEFLOOR THUNDERSTORM: Land of the Free, Home of the Rave

THE
RAVER STORIES
PROJECT

Produced and Edited by

Michael Tullberg

Stories written by various authors; compilation and editing by Michael Tullberg

Additional editing by Steve Stoliar

THE RAVER
STORIES
PROJECT

Produced and edited by
MICHAEL TULLBERG

© 2017 by 5150 Publishing, Inc.
P.O. Box 86802
Los Angeles, CA 90086 USA

All rights reserved

Non-fiction; First Edition

ISBN #: 978-0-9971070-1-2

LCCN: 2017906600

ACKNOWLEDGMENTS

The publishers would like to thank the following people and organizations for their support and assistance: Steve Stoliar, Susan Mainzer, Linda Nuanluoong, Danny D'Brito, Mark Lewis, Paul Oakenfold, Jason Blakemore, Holly Adams, Sarah Polonsky, Josh Glazer, Rob Simas, Insomniac Productions, MagneticMag.com, Duncan Dick, Mixmag, Christopher Lawrence, Sara Finlayson, Wade Hampton, Raymond Roker, Janine Jordan, Lauren Segal, Chris Ellington, Sven and Kathleen Tullberg, Frank and Nancy DiMella, Kent Damon, Margaret Schlamp, Gina & Richard Risemberg, Getty Images' Los Angeles division, all the IndieGogo crowdfunding supporters who were ever so generous, all of the contributing authors who did such a great job, and most especially, all of the ravers, promoters, producers and artists who made all of this possible in the first place.

TABLE OF CONTENTS

Dune 4 Desert Rave. Photo: Michael Tullberg.

INTRODUCTION

The rave scene is filled with all sorts of people, and all have different stories. It is a diversity that mirrors the best aspects of this country, and that is not an accident.

When I began covering the American rave scene in the mid-1990s, I was immediately struck by the unique sense of participation in the scene by the fans themselves. This was unlike any other social scene I had witnessed before, and I had seen plenty. The rave scene was different, in that the fans were just as an important part of this pop culture equation as the artists were. It allowed the near-total freedom of self-expression, in terms of fashion, musical taste, and of course, dance. You could literally do anything on the dance floor. You could *be* anything on the dance floor, and you wouldn't be judged or belittled. The rave scene eliminated the barriers of class, social status, race and sexuality, and since it also had the best beats on the planet, there were glorious opportunities to celebrate life through dance.

However, traditionally the voices of the fans of electronic music have been overlooked by the mainstream media, who have instead chosen to focus mostly on the various controversies surrounding the scene, usually in a very negatively slanted fashion. You know the old saying: "if it bleeds, it leads." I consider this to be deeply unfair, because it is the fans who are the backbone of any scene or movement. You can have the best DJs in the world at a party, but if no one is there dancing to their music, all those DJs are doing is playing for each other. In the final analysis, it is the fans who ultimately make a music or social scene possible, be it rave, rock, hip-hop, jazz, whatever.

Back in the day, magazines like *URB* and *Lotus* performed the function of letting the fans air their views and experiences. Very often stories would appear in these publications that bore a distinct resemblance to some found in this book. Sadly, those magazines are no more, which is one of the reasons why this collection has been assembled. A group that has grown and evolved as successfully as the rave scene has over the last twenty-five years does not deserve to be simply singled out and dismissed by those who do not understand why these people do what they do.

Some of the stories within are of one night. Others cover years of their author's life. Both are legitimate, for they show how peoples' lives are affected by the rave scene, both in the short-term and lifelong. Some events are epic, and some are more pedestrian in nature.

Both the old-school rave and EDM generations are represented, because both are part of the greater history of this scene, and therefore both must be represented. From Josh Wink and Paul Oakenfold to the Chainsmokers and Skrillex, from vinyl to CDs to laptops, from warehouses to stadiums…it's all part of the same overall story, and the individual tales are the bricks that make up this big, beautiful house.

We have parties in all sorts of locations included here. We start with the original acid house explosion in England in the late '80s, and wrap up in the modern EDM world of today. There are massive stadium gigs like Electric Daisy Carnival, and the ultimate counter-culture celebration,

Burning Man. There are parties in the desert, in huge mansions, and in secret warehouses. We have young EDM writers barely out of their teens, and old-school rave veterans pushing middle age. These are more than just partyers—they're representatives from a unique era in pop culture history, telling how the rave scene grew, thrived and survived against no small amount of adversity.

The opinions of the writers who have contributed to this project are their own, and some may seem to contradict others. That's fine, because the rave scene is not a unified bloc. People from different places and times are naturally going to have different experiences. However, there are shared elements in the scene that touch these different people: acceptance, tolerance, liberation, happiness, wonder, and yes, even transcendence. These are the rave scene's great unifiers.

I think that it is very telling that the fans of this music have often sought out the rave scene as a sanctuary from the troubles and traumas of their lives. It is the warm, embracing and healing properties of the scene that make this possible, as you will see in the testimonies here. Many uninformed people have all too regularly regarded the electronic music world solely as a haven for drug abuse. The stories in this volume show that this beat-driven haven offers much more than that blinkered, narrow viewpoint. The scene has helped save some of those featured in this book from the ravages of gang life, domestic abuse and suicidal thoughts. It has launched professional careers and opened previously closed minds to new ideas and philosophies. It has allowed those in it the freedom to find their own identities, away from the frequently judgmental and adversarial atmosphere of the everyday world. For these alone, the rave scene deserves a more even-minded and sober reevaluation by those not in it.

Throughout the process of assembling this book, great lengths have been taken to ensure that the voices in these pieces remain true to their authors, and from the beginning the editors have been determined not to rewrite them in their own style. Whatever changes that have been made have been strictly for the improvement of readability. No facts, quotes or figures were altered. All revisions were made with the full knowledge and approval of the authors, who were fully engaged in the evolution of their pieces, from the time they submitted their original drafts to the final polishing up.

It has been a privilege to go through these stories. They truly show the strength and character of the people within this scene, and they have also reminded me why I've been a part of this community for so long. I hope that you enjoy them as much as I have, as we now slip back in time to this amazing era in pop culture.

–Michael Tullberg, Los Angeles, California

1 PHILIP HILTON - STERNS, UK ('89)

Philip Hilton is a yoga enthusiast who experienced the original late 1980s UK rave explosion as a regular at the now-legendary Sterns nightclub in Worthing.

Welcome to Fantasia: the world of magic, love, rave, music and dancing.

This is my story, the story of rave.

The story starts in Hull, Humberside for me in the north of England where I grew up on soul, jazz, funk, and hip-hop, and spent the '80s breakdancing in the under-18s soul clubs. Then, something wonderful started happening: the birth of the acid-house scene. Acid is not a drug—it's a miracle phenomenon of dance music that captivated a whole generation. People still live up to this period with dress, style and musical inspiration. It was the beginnings of a great event in history, the biggest movement ever... yes, the house music rave scene.

We finally had a voice, and a new religion had begun.

I grew up with the terrible gang football hooliganism that was ever-present in the '80s (mostly alcohol fueled), and I witnessed something magical happening. Along came rave and the football hooliganism practically stopped overnight, right across Britain. All the hooligans wanted to do is dance and party to this new exciting music, and so they did. Many of the raves were run by the now ex-hooligans, so we can thank UK rave and the house music scene for giving us a flipping miracle in Britain. Nothing else could have the power to stop the whole of Britain's hooligan wars, but rave did where Maggie Thatcher couldn't.

My first rave was at an acid-house gig in Hull. I didn't dance much, as we all took some magic mushrooms…never really took them too much ever again after that night. Music is what's important here; we have to believe that to keep rave real and true. After that night, I started attending acid-house raves at the Adelphi club in Hull…such fantastic crazy memories! All I remember was being on the dance floor surrounded by intense smoke where you couldn't see a thing, apart from flashing colours. Oh, the laughs we had…

But this was just the beginning of an awesome journey for me and millions of others. Yes, we are ravers and proud of it. God, I put a lot of time and effort and energy into my time on the dance floor, so why not be proud of our history? It's our life story, and what a story it is!

So from the branches of acid house came UK rave. For me living in Britain, it all started in Chicago: the roots of house music, dance music, with the likes of DJ Frankie Knuckles, the Godfather of house. House started because people [there] were into a new dance vibe mostly played at gay clubs and the records you could get from a place called the house, so people where always asking for the latest house music label. It's purely simple truth—from Chicago, the music started hitting Britain slowly, but it was the genius of a group of lads at a football match one day that changed everything. They knew of Chicago house music surfacing and they went to

Ibiza and loved the new dance music scene there so much, so they decided to bring the experience back to the UK and opened a club first rave playing this new strange cool music that literally made people dance. From there, the rest is history.

I sadly missed the first rave summer of love eruption in '88, as I was working on holiday camps on the Isle of Wight as a chef, until I got back onto mainland Britain, where rave was quickly overtaking my boring life. Well it was, wasn't it? Once you experience rave…you are different and your life is different, definitely more exciting. We ravers have always got something good and cool to say; we lived the dream.

When I was settled on a new holiday camp job working near Chichester at a place called Wittering, I did the most awesome thing. Me and my friends found a flyer in a pub for a rave at a club called Sterns in Worthing, so we said, "Bollocks, let's get a Sterns membership." So we ran nearly to the record shop to get our membership, and this was the vital turning point in my rave history. The rave scene was first called dance-music scene and was known as hardcore. Now, Sterns was so addictive, which is why I spent nearly four years going every single week, apart from raves we visited elsewhere. Sterns is my rave club, my home, my magic, my memories, my life. The place was very special, magical. Picture this: Sterns was an old 18th-century mansion turned into a rave club with three floors. It was situated on this big hill with nothing else on it, just one road leading up to Sterns itself. It was so freaking cool seeing the motorway full of cars, and especially the cars that lit up the dark road leading to Sterns. And wow, the Hill is a special place, especially with the Druids who sometimes hold rituals on Highdown Hill. Sterns was called "house on the hill" for that reason.

We all came out of Sterns one morning after an all-nighter on Easter, and everyone was giggling as hundreds of Druids were walking up the hill. We cheekily laughed to say, "If you only knew what we was doing in that club!" Sterns, what a blast of a party, ha!

Sterns was nominated the best club in Europe…so much so [that] people are bringing out the first rave movie about Sterns and its totally rad intelligent cool groovy, people. It's called "Mensa Lord of the Dance."

I spent so much time dancing at Sterns, especially in the Underground. This was a basement room [that was] quite big, in Sterns itself. You walked to the doors to the main dance floor—this is where the magic happened, believe you me. It was called the Underground and had a London Underground sign above the door, which led you to a big flight of stairs with huge mirrors on either side of the walls. The stairs led to the basement dance floor, and I loved it down there. I met my son's mum there and fell in love, especially in the second summer of love [of] '91. This was the year all-nighters were legalized in the UK, which was a fantastic move—party on, dudes! Once you're in party-rave mode, you party for days…dancing was so addictive, and still is.

Sterns had over 10,000 members, but could only hold a couple of thousand, so MENSA (the owner) set up a massive rave to hold all Sterns members. This took place in Brighton in '91, called "Brighton Dance 91." The night was fantastic, mind blowing, a total rave success. I remember Rat Pack was there, the lasers were spectacular. I'm a really big fan of lasers at raves and I hope to own a system one day soon. I'm an artist and much of my digital computer-created art is inspired by lasers and the rave scene called my rave art.

I was quite famous at Sterns. Apart from being a regular face, I was called the Vicks Man, as back in '90 I met someone at Sterns and they were from the Raindance raves, and they had some Vicks VapoRub usually for blocked noses, but this guy and his partner rubbed some on my face and told me to stand in front of the huge base speakers, which I did, and I became overwhelmed by a cool feeling and the base speakers were blowing air onto your face creating a cooling effect, as boy oh boy, it was hot and sweaty down in the Underground. The ceiling used to rain sweat onto people—it [was] all the intense dancing energy. I used to be known for taking weird toys (illuminous stuff) to Sterns, totally bonkers-conkers but brilliant.

I had a superb night-one rave at Sterns on my 21st birthday and it fell on an all-nighter. It was a dream come true and the night was the best, as Mr C of the band the Shamen was playing an awesome DJ set and my brother was an MC at raves. He TRIED (bless him) but couldn't get first dibs to appear at lots of raves. A hard business to be in, he just didn't get the big break. He was amazing. I was so proud of him seeing him on stage controlling the crowd. Sadly, my younger MC brother passed away from cancer at 41 recently. Such a tragic loss to the family: such a clever, talented man, especially with rapping, MCing and songwriting. Most of my family are musicians in bands; we love music, our family.

I'm a big fan of the raves called Fantasia. These are big events like Helter Skelter and Dreamscape raves. Most are 100,000+. If you love rave, then you have to watch the Fantasia raves on YouTube. If you look, there is a groovy awesome collection of UK raves available. Tune in now, ravers!

Now I would like to cast my words of wisdom and knowledge to you, in regards to some people (or many people) taking the dance drug Ecstasy. Now I have to be honest: I did take E at raves, for it was better and safer than alcohol. Ecstasy was once legal for a time in Switzerland—the doctors would give it to people who were arguing, as the drug made people loved up with no worries, and the rave scene picked up on that and the drug became part of rave history. I'm not here to encourage drug taking... Yes, it was fun (best time ever!), but after five years of taking it, I became a bit depressed, and people have died, though not as much as alcohol, which kills thousands and thousands every year. I personally wouldn't take it again, especially while it's illegal and dangerous, as you don't know where they're coming from. [It] could be created by the Taliban. If that was [true that] drugs come from terrorists, you wouldn't do it nor encourage it.

Anyway, I don't need that anymore. Music and dancing is where it's at, and if we have to rely on some drug, then the rave scene means nothing, okay?

The way forward for the rave scene is yoga, believe it or not, as scientists have discovered that yoga releases the same chemicals as the dance drug Ecstasy into the brain, but the chemicals are released in a safe quantity and in their proper order, giving you a clear-minded altered state of being. Yoga is very powerful: it releases and produces the same chemicals and energies as the human orgasm, which is why we yogis smile a lot. I have been studying and doing yoga for 20 years now. Yoga is the way forward for us ravers; we are called yoga ravers. Yoga raving is the new big craze taking off in the USA and UK.

So ravers, that's just a sample of my rave history and memories. Hope you enjoyed the history lesson. Just remember, never stop the rave people, and keep on believing all the dreams inside of you.

Lastly, I'm a big fan of the garage scene since '92.

Love piano rave music and rave songs with vocals in them. Blows your soul away. THANK YOU ravers, this is Fantasia, love you all.

BROSTAR Philip

2 COCKROACH - UK ('90)

Cockroach took part in the original UK Acid House explosion of the late 1980s, before becoming inspired to be an electronic music producer.

Growing up through punk and the Eighties street-punk movement in the UK, listening to bands like Crass, Discharge, and The Exploited, it was a totally surreal experience first entering a club where nobody was drinking and everybody was united around a brand new vibe, focused around a brand new music. Little did I know this strange yet exciting music was to be my key, one to a different world.

Every youth movement has a beginning point. Start something, people enjoy it, and pretty soon other people will want to join in. I totally fell into a scene that was erupting throughout Britain, and predictably, scare tactics in the press about illegal raves and a nation in the grip of E meant the mainstream would never understand. I got it; it was people dancing, it was people uniting, and it was partying like never before.

However, if the kids are loving it, normally the authorities are seeing it another way, and it's a shame they were too blinkered to see the bigger picture: a picture of violence slowing on the streets and in the clubs, heralding an unprecedented fusion of youth cultures. There was a time you could tell what someone was into and if he was on your side just by the way they looked. He's got a leather jacket with studs on, must be a punk rocker; he's got a parka, he's a Mod. All of these old divisions were disappearing; the youth of the country were starting to congeal together into a uniformed force without a uniform, even though that would change.

At this point, it was just raving. There wasn't the "I'm into this and your into that" attitude. It was just thousands of people every weekend wanting to go out and party, *and what's wrong with that?* I hear you ask. It's a crazy, crazy world, my friend, and "let's have it" was my approach to this brave new world I had stumbled upon one Friday night after taking my first E, a Dove, remember them? I'm not trying to big up drugs—we all experience things through our lives. My life's mine, your life's yours, but I knew that small white twenty-quid pill had changed my life forever. I didn't want no alcohol, didn't see the world in a closed way, but saw it as us, together.

The next day, I bumped into an old school friend at Scarborough train station, who by coincidence had taken the same pill in a different town the night before. This meeting set the stage for me travelling up and down the UK, partying at the best clubs the globe had to offer. From dancing on top of 30-foot speakers and feeling like a superstar to being chased by the police in helicopters, these were my halcyon days of rave; big enough to be accessible, but small enough to make you feel you were part of an elite gang of rebels living outside of society.

It felt like the whole country was gonna explode as the underground began to erupt into the mainstream, growing on a scale that no one could have expected. The bloke next door was suddenly your raver friend, never mind the person you never met before at gigs like Raindance or Techno-drome. People who would have been fighting at football on a Saturday afternoon were hanging out together taking pills, appreciating music, and making friends.

I looked at the scene and the way it was proliferating society and I thought, "Join in," and they did. All over the country, new clubs sprang up and no longer was it illegal warehouse parties. The money men had stepped in to seize the chance to cash in on the growing scene, with tents, fairground rides, mass security and ticket prices getting silly. The events got bigger, and more and more people joined the party. It was happening on a scale that the authorities hadn't estimated...which inevitably produced a reaction from them that was totally overblown.

When the draconian Criminal Justice Bill became law in 1994, it officially enforced the idea that people gathering together enjoying themselves and being free to do what they choose would be illegal. I thought it was time to fight back and started growing a vibe of my own.

Having been in various bands in my teens, I took the do-it-yourself, anything-is-possible approach of punk that the rave scene shared, and began making tunes myself. I applied for a grant from the Foundation for Sport Arts and bought myself a workstation keyboard, Akai sampler, a mixer and monitors. After getting to know the equipment I had acquired inside out, I set about teaching myself about MIDI and began to use Cubase as a sequencer on a computer.

The name Cockroach was born out of the idea of survival, still being around when everything else had gone. I began designing flyers for lager raves under the name Insomniak while organizing events with friends,

DJing, hiring our own lasers, rigs and sound systems. I converted my garage into a studio, complete with its own chill-out area. After receiving positive feedback on the early tracks I recorded from the music magazines of the day (including Future Music and Sound on Sound, who both awarded me Demo of the Month on a regular basis), I released an album called "Infestation" on my own Insomniak label. Cockroach is still going strong today, and with an album deal in the USA and a deal in Australia, it's gone global.

These were my memories of the rave scene, in those days anyhow—the good times, the unity, and the people all made the scene so special at that time. After that, when we would go to clubs, things seemed different, the scene was splintering into factions. In the early days, it was just people going out partying; now it seemed like a million different names for the same music were coming into it; drum and bass, techno, trance, hard house…the list goes on and on. Everyone turning elitist, "I'm not into that, I'm into this." The same thing happened with punk; it split people up and made sure they started bickering amongst themselves and forgetting why they were into it in the first place.

The electronic music scene is growing bigger by the year. My message to you is: Be part of it, keep it real, and I hope you enjoy it as much as I did.

LOVE, PEACE & RESPECT, FOREVER.

3 ROBBIE HARDKISS - NYC ('92)

DJ Robbie Hardkiss has been spinning incredible sets for more than two decades.

(Originally posted on social media. Rewritten and printed here with permission of the author.)

In remembering my friend Scott Hardkiss on his birthday today, here's the funny little story of a trip we took to New York when we were in high school...

We told our parents that we were going to New York to visit NYU, which I was considering for college. Not true. I mean, I was considering it, and we did walk around Washington Square Park, but we were not there to visit any college. We went there to visit The Limelight, Palladium and any other dance clubs we could find and get into.

The first thing we two young'uns needed was fake IDs. Scott was really into art and familiar with graphic-design tools, so he thought that we could use Chartpak press-on letters and numbers to go over our existing driver's licenses and change our birthdates. It was a painstaking process, and we weren't able to finish before hopping on Amtrak from DC to NYC. We tried to finish on the train, but that was even more difficult, with all the wobbling and shaking on the tracks.

When we got to Penn Station, we jumped on the subway up to my aunt and uncle's apartment on 105th and Broadway. We were afraid to tell them that we were making fake IDs, which is funny now, because I don't think they would've minded. In fact, I'm pretty sure they would've been proud and wanted to go out with us! But we needed someplace to work, so we headed back downtown, where we would eventually be going out. We went to a library for a while, but got spooked about breaking the law with all those people around. We then started working on them at a bench in Union Square, where one of us would work while the other would look out for cops. I'm not kidding! We really thought the police might bust us... That is some seriously sheltered, suburban good-boy paranoia right there. So, so funny. Well, we couldn't finish the job there either. We had to keep moving. We eventually finished them in a restaurant bathroom in Chinatown, where we had dinner. One of us ate while the other went to the bathroom to finish his ID. Didn't attract any attention from the authorities there, but I'm pretty sure the wait staff thought we were doing cocaine in there. They were happy to give us the check and we were happy and nervous to go see if our IDs would work.

We went to the Palladium first, which was one of Steve Rubell and Ian Schrager's post-Studio 54 ventures. We were both wearing long wool coats. I mention that because it makes me chuckle a bit that I'm 48 now and haven't had a coat that "adult" since then. It was really early in the night, so the line wasn't that long. I remember nervously walking up to the velvet rope, handing the bouncer my ID, and having him pull back the rope and wave me in. *It worked!* It only took about 10 seconds. We were in!

When we got all the way into the huge, multi-level main room, the DJ, whose name I can't recall because I didn't know to care or check back then, was playing Kraftwerk's "The Telephone Call." I remember, because I was psyched. I had the cassette at home. We followed the song out onto the dance floor and listened to the biggest club sound system I had ever heard. It was dark in the club, but surrounding the dance floor was what looked like three stories of big stacked blocks that lit up and changed colors. There were bass bins in the corners with people dancing on them, multiple disco balls, and large grid-like groupings of television screens flashing images.

Just off of the dance floor were various lounge areas. We walked around trying to find girls to chat up. I felt like a foreigner. I had been to a couple of small clubs in DC, but nothing like this. We went to the bar for some liquid courage. I asked for a Heineken...It was $8.00. What!? I think I actually said, "For a six-pack?" No, just one beer. It was 1987, way before $20 drinks, but still pretty extortionate. I was disappointed with the realization of how few drinks I was going to be able to afford that night. I was also disappointed with my failure to connect with any females. I don't think Scott was doing any better, so we decided to bail and check out The Limelight.

By this time, it was late enough for the velvet rope at The Limelight to be packed. No line, just a mass of people trying to show that they had the look, the money, or the breasts to get in. There we were, two high-school boys from Maryland in long coats with very little game and very little money, trying to get picked. Needless to say, it was not going well. We thought maybe if we spoke French, they'd think we were cool and let us in. Neither of us spoke French, but we could speak fake French, so that's what we did for a while. We were cracking ourselves up. Of course, it didn't work, but at least we were having fun at this point.

We saw that every girl that came up was allowed in, so we started talking to some of them. We kind of made a connection with a couple—I think our French was making them laugh, too. So when they got picked, we followed as though we were with them. But right after the second girl crossed the threshold, clank: the sound of metal as the rope closed in front of us. We hollered at the girls, but they never even looked back. We did eventually get in after another hour or so out in the cold. Not sure we would've lasted that long without our fancy coats. Once inside, I ordered my second (and last) $8 beer of the night. We never did hook up with any girls that night, but we danced, yapped and cracked each other up like we always did. Who knew that in just a few years, Scott and I would be flown in from San Francisco to DJ in that very same club? No fake French needed at the velvet rope that night! I bet we still did it though.

I miss those days. I miss my friend.

Scott and Robbie Hardkiss, graduation photo.

4 ROSA COSTANZA - A NEW YORKER ON A MISSION IN LOS ANGELES ('92)

Rosa is a Film and TV Producer who has produced films, music videos, Grammy selected music albums and international events.

My techno-tinged story begins in 1992. Was it an underground warehouse party that was permitted, hmmm, or an outlaw event where it was breaking and entering? I went. If the party was in a club, it was assumedly an over-18 age requirement, in which case I would not have the identification necessary. Getting in to parties in NYC was always a mission of some sort for me.

I really didn't need any ID most of the time, because I knew Drag artists and Club Kids who hosted parties at the best spots in the greater New York area, where ravers mingled with disco babies of the '70s, electronica fans of the '80s, and all the NYC '90s glitterati. Save The Robots. The Limelight. Palladium. Club USA. The Tunnel. Twilo. The Roxy. Light, Wisdom & Sound. Nells. The Shelter. The Cooler. Vault. Roseland Ballroom. So many amazing venues, full of such talent.

Electronic music and raver fashion drew me into the scene, along with an invite to go to a rave with my high-school best friend. We trooped to a Satellite event called Sputnik in upstate New York where we lived. She and I sat and stared at the lights, mesmerized. We marveled at the freedom of expression evident in the kids around us, in contrast to the conformity of culture in upstate. We thrilled with the joy of dancing, here a sudden ability to escape the monotony of high-school life. I continued to seek out the local upstate raves, until they weren't enough for me. I dove straight into the rabbit hole in The City.

The author in her NYC years. Photo unknown.

My affinity for house and techno parties in Manhattan was cemented by my employment as a promoter for a lighting company from upstate, Acme. The Acme guys had rolled up to my house one day and asked if I would be in their crew. I had lists of stores to drop flyers off at and was paid to troop around NYC record shops, clothing stores, and any rave life-style hangouts during the day. At night, I handed out their flyers at clubs and rave parties and became a fixture on guest lists. I felt part of a community, something that I hadn't achieved in school.

I networked my way into the super clubs at night and was rarely asked my age, because I was styled right. I hung out at Patricia Field's East Eighth Street shop House of Field, daytime; lounged around Liquid Sky's Lafayette Street clothing store, scoring styles from the mavens, Chloë Sevigny and Carisa Barah; listened to vinyl downstairs at Temple Records. I frequented all the record shops checking cuts, like Sonic Groove, Satellite Records, and Breakbeat Science. I bought wardrobe at *anime* shops and SoHo boutiques. My immersion in the rave world of the greater NYC area was maximized. I was all about it from age 15 onwards. I learned to DJ; had a turntable teacher. I was building up a vinyl collection. But through no fault of my own, my life veered from that course.

In 1994, I ended up in Southern California; why is a sidebar conversation. I was living in Ventura for a spell. There really was scarcely a rave culture there, but I still managed to meet the underground heads (you know who you are in the 805!), mainly punks and ska heads. I met S.C. in Ventura: he was an amazing illustrator and graphic designer who drew the same style of rave cartoons as I did: Graffiti-style bubbly kids with baggy clothes; big, bug-eyed girls with little clothes; aliens, always. The rave culture's tag-style artwork connected us as much as the music. I was so excited when he asked me one day to go to an underground party in Los Angeles, as I had no contact with the L.A. scene except to see DJs like Doc Martin in the parties back east.

I had come from NYC to live in the sleepy surfer punk squatter town of Ventura all of a sudden and against my will, so I was in severe need of going to a good rave. My new friend, S.C., had a flyer with a smiley face at the top and directions to an intersection. There was a time frame to arrive to this location, Map Point #01, or all was lost. Do not pass Go.

It was still dusk when our hunt began. Map Point #1 was an unassuming street corner. We parked a few blocks away and walked nonchalantly, S.C. being adamant that we stay covert and not call attention to the location; a typical mission to go to certain parties under the radar in Los Angeles, apparently. S.C. told me that if we didn't look and behave right, we may be rejected and not get the party coordinates. High stakes. I loved every minute of it. There was an organic quality alongside the novelty; L.A. was not yet as popularized as the scene I had left in New York. It was fresh. We met two people, a guy and a girl, on the intersection corner; we passed scrutiny and left with new instructions.

We hit Map Point #2, and from there we had the map and other details to get to this warehouse. It was in an industrial area in downtown L.A. We parked on an adjacent street and walked a few blocks, as S.C. didn't want his car near the venue. I remember this detail, because I loved the platform sneakers I wore that night, Pumas. I had brought them with me from New York; the layers of added sole cushioned my trek to the venue and brought me closer to the stars than my usual 5'4" could.

I was caught off-guard by the amount of people who had all managed to find this venue, just as we had. The flyer-map point-adventure trek to get directions worked well.

Walking in, we got hit with a wave of sound and I marveled at the speaker stacks. The amount of sound gear that was set up caught my DJ apprentice mind's attention. Also, I remember being impressed at how many people could dance on top of the speakers, in addition to the rumble of the dynamic range emitted by the stacks.

Just as in New York, there were creatively attired ravers who fell into certain easily recognizable categories. The ultra-styled and unique Club Kids; the sporty B-Boys and B-Girls, some in tracksuits; the Goths/Industrial heads for whom black is the new black; the scantily clad of either gender, the androgynous...the usual rave-flavored assortment of fashion experimentation.

We journeyed back to the main floor and danced. S.C. was in his zone. I was impressed with the fruit salad bar that was being operated at the party and had to go there. They had mounds of watermelon, oranges and more. It was remarkably more fruit than I had ever seen at a New York party, where I was used to smoothie-making "Smart Bars." I downed some melon and then hit the dance floor again.

All of a sudden, the place was raided by the fire department and some shouting and screaming started. S.C. was still in his dance trance. I got him to be alert quickly, though, grabbing his arm, saying we had to exit through the descent of chaos. S.C. stopped me from joining the crowd headed out the front exit and took us back into the venue instead of out.

We headed towards the DJ booth. The Hardkiss Brothers, Moontribe crew...there were a few people he knew, and so we ended up getting co-ordinates for the next phase of the party, an impromptu after-party at a house in L.A. This turned out to be the house belonging to Moontribe DJ John Kelley.

S.C. had thought ahead of time about the possibility of having to make a break for it and escape the venue. High as he definitely was, he did snap to it really quick. I was then thankful that he had wisely parked a few blocks away and not in the parking lot adjacent to the warehouse. We got back to his car and he managed to get us to the after party, no problem. There were turntables and speakers already set up in the living room when we got there, while more P.A. equipment and record crates got moved in.

Another form of camaraderie occurs when you and your crew have to flee a warehouse as it gets shut down. You know what I mean? I had been in a massive New Year's Eve warehouse rave in Brooklyn that was busted up, where thousands of people poured onto the streets and into the subways. In that case, my friends and I made our way to the home of a crew called Half Baked and continued the festivities.

However, in early '90s Los Angeles, the rave world seemed not to have infiltrated the big club venues as in NYC, so my impression was that L.A. ravers sustained this vulnerable state of outlaw-ism, something that made it all the more special and compelling. Our myth back east was that the L.A. kids partied in the desert, something exotic and mystical. (This was before Burning Man.) To a New Yorker who was used to living in an industrial surrounding, the idea of raving in nature was truly far out.

Back to L.A... it was early in the morning, maybe 4:00 AM. Before sunrise. I was lounging on a couch, writing a letter to my best friend at the time, Tamara. She lived in Little Neck on Long Island and I often visited her there so we could go to caffeine parties. I wanted to tell her about this adventure in the wild wild west. I wrote my story to her on part of a page and was doodling a cartoon raver kid on the bottom, when Scott Hardkiss came over and asked what I was up to. I asked him to tag the bottom of the letter, near my raver art. He wrote his own note, too. Way cooler than asking for an autograph.

I knew that Tamara was going to freak out once she got the letter. She and I were total technophiles. We had a 'zine, called XING, in which we wrote about music, made show reviews, articles on related topics, our doodles, fortune-cookie wisdoms, rave flyer reprints, reader submissions... the usual. Tamara had a friend who owned a printing press and was into our "punk rock" publication. He ran our two editions of the zine, which we handed out at clubs and at rave parties. There I was, reporting back to Tamara in Long Island from the west coast, documenting this epic California party night.

The rave underground in early '90s L.A. had a special sparkling charm from then on for me. It has not lost this quality, twenty-plus years later. Back then, I had gone on a hunt to get the location coordinates, had found and enjoyed the event. Though cut short by authorities, we escaped, no problem, and ended up at a cozy intimate after-hours at John Kelley's house.

Whenever I go out to L.A. parties now, I still feel like I am on a mission, likely thanks to this introductory experience. Every musically curated evening I have here is an adventure, holding the possibility of unimaginable fun, of connection with friends through music and through love. At least I can bring that deep connection wherever I go, and lift the energy and spirit around me by reasserting my extreme joy to be a part of this exciting time and place.

5 ARIKA "KOKO" SANTOS - LOS ANGELES ('94)

Arika Santos is an artist of many mediums, including murals, painting, drawing, sculpture, jewelry design, dance, poetry and fashion/costume design.

I know deep in my soul that I would not be the person I am today had I not experienced the underground rave scene in the mid '90s. I was exposed to the underground through the Latin Deep House scene and Ditching Parties. I still remember playing cassette tapes of underground electronic music on my Walkman. The first tape I had, "Jungle" on one side and "Hardcore" on the B side, was given to me by a guy I dated named "Asid," who was a skater/raver. I was in love with him and the music before I actually attended my first rave. It was a warehouse party called Aphrodisiac in Los Angeles, in 1994 or '95. I spent the night at a friend's house, then snuck out and ran through some neighbor's yard as dogs chased me. The first thing I did, once I escaped, was call the info line to get directions, then I had to call my ride from a payphone in the middle of South Central Los Angeles. It was definitely sketchy, but so exciting.

Even though in the mid '90s, the underground scene was starting to dwindle, I am so grateful that I caught the tail end of the dirty, dingy, warehouse parties. What I loved about the scene back then was the vibe itself. It was all about the vibe. It was soulful, communal and full of love. Everything from the music, the drugs, the people, the location, all fit together and harmonized in a way that was simply magical! The vibe was more than the general feel of the party; it was the heart and soul of the party. It was like a living entity that came alive and brought us together at just the right moment, like the stars were in alignment somehow. There were many different sub-categories like trance, house, tribal, jungle, techno, drum and bass, but we all got along and had such a blast dancing and raving till the break of dawn.

I liked jungle and drum and bass, but my true love was Hardcore Techno. This style of music and ambiance was just what I needed as a troubled youth growing up in Los Angeles. Growing up in the '90s was intense on many levels, especially being raised by a single parent. I faced hardships such as abandonment, poverty, abuse, and also witnessed many social injustices such as police brutality and the L.A. Riots. "No justice. No peace" was a common phrase in L.A. at the time. There was an aggressiveness in the fast-paced BPM that was absolutely exhilarating. I would mosh and climb the speakers, sometimes diving into the crowd. I feel like we were kind of the outcasts and punks of the underground rave scene. If it was a party with multiple rooms, we always had the dirtiest, darkest and dingiest area tucked away in a basement or corner. I was called a speaker whore, because I worshipped those big black speakers. When the bass rushed, it was like I was making love or fucking the speaker!!

I was very petite in size, but always held it down in my space right in front of the speakers, even when it got super-rough, which it did. I liked the roughness and moshing to the pounding bass in my face, but what I loved about the old-school vibe was when the music slowed down and the bass took a break and we all took a break, too, hugging each other with our arms shoulder to shoulder. Then the bass would start again and we would chant in unison, "Mutha-fucking hardcore," some of us blowing whistles to the beat. We would all be on the same vibe and same beat, bouncing side to side, embracing each other and the music. We worshipped the music. We worshipped the speaker like it was our God.

Psychedelics definitely enhanced our holy moments with the music and vibe. They opened my psyche and showed me many places in my mind that I'd never explored. It opened doors to new perceptions I never experienced before. The visuals, along with the music, black lights, digital projections, smoke machines, people and general vibe of the party all enhanced my trips like I was in a symphony. Everything related to each other and harmonized in a very authentic and beautiful way. It all flowed together like an orchestra with many instruments coming together to create something that simply couldn't exist without all sections and instruments playing together at the right moment, vibe and energy. Even though there was so much outer stimulation, the true magic came as an internal longing and feeling like I was home. The more open I was, the more I explored and experienced, the conductor was actually me. I love how life was orchestrated to me through the rave scene.

Although I loved acid, it was never fully about the drugs for me. I even recall being sober at a few parties, just because I loved the music so much. I also loved how close the DJs were back then. They usually played at the same level as the crowd and interacted a lot with us. We were all on the same level and same vibe. It wasn't like the later days of massives, where the DJs had stages or platforms. Although we had mad respect for the DJs, there was no hierarchy. You could actually reach out and give them a high-five or a hug in between vinyl sets. They were very approachable. The DJs were more like the messengers. The speakers and the music were what we truly worshipped, not the DJs themselves.

There was just so much love. Love and acceptance everywhere. It was like a whole other world when I was at a party. I saw and met so many different types of people and loved them all. In the underground underworld, you were free to be unique and be yourself. We accepted others for being who they were. From the elaborate costumes of the drag Club Kids, to gay people openly making out and being themselves, to witnessing huge orgies just out in public, it opened me up at the age of 14 to being very tolerant and accepting of all. All walks of life were accepted and there were no color lines, socio-economic, gender or homophobic tendencies. A stranger could just walk up to you and you could hug them and connect in a way that was so authentic and different from the city streets, where people often didn't even give eye contact, let alone start a conversation or give free hugs openly. It contrasted the harshness of city life, and was so refreshing because L.A. in the '90s had an uproar with Rodney King and the L.A. Riots, gang activity, race riots at schools, drive-by shootings and tons of violence. This is why creating an environment based on Peace, Love, Unity and Respect was so vital and necessary for us at the time. It was truly magical and revolutionary. Ravers were like the modern-day hippies. Free love. Free to be yourself. Free to be accepted. Erasing the color lines and stopping the violence through this way of life.

Being a person who has always loved fashion and freedom of expression, I absolutely loved dressing up to go to parties. I was what you would call a candy kid. I remember planning out my outfits weeks before a party. Going to thrift shops to find cool unique vintage clothes with bright and broad patterns and colors and prints, soccer shirts, golf pants and whatever else was different and unique. I also used to sew my own clothes and add glow-in-the-dark stars or puffy paint that would look cool under the black lights. I used a ton of glitter everywhere!! On my face, especially my cheeks, and in my hair. My hair was usually done up in ponytails, or Princess Leia buns, or braids. I never wore my hair down, because I needed to stay cool, while I was sweating and dancing for hours, so my hair had to be out of my face and off my neck. I adorned my hair with ribbons, barrettes, fuzzy pompoms and tons of glitter.

I also loved Adidas jackets and white gloves, which looked cool when I danced and pop-blocked with the black lights and visuals. I made backpacks out of cereal boxes or Tide laundry detergent boxes, which were full of goodies and necessities for the night. I packed things like gum and sour candy to share, weird trippy toys to trip out on, more glitter and stickers, a disposable film camera, and a sketchbook with markers, because I was a graffiti artist and always wanted to get other people to tag or draw in my black book, and also to write down phone numbers of the people that I would meet, because back then we didn't have cell phones.

I love how unique our style was back then. It was really a lot about originality. We created our looks from scrap. By the next morning, my cute DIY costumes and clothing I'd planned out and sewed were usually rags and falling apart. I danced so hard for hours that my creations literally fell apart at the seams—I busted out! That's how I knew it was a dope party. That, and the black boogers from dancing with all the dust from the warehouses.

Another highlight of raving in the '90s was the map points! I loved the anticipation leading up to the warehouse parties, especially because you never knew the exact location of the event. Prior to the map point, all you had on the flyer was a number to call on the night of the event, and that number would lead you to a voicemail that would lead you to the map point. Sometimes there were multiple checkpoints and codes, because back then, many underground parties were in illegal, abandoned warehouses and the map points helped to weed out undercover cops, posers and negative vibes. It was like a pirate map to seek the treasure that sometimes had many obstacles along the way.

The secret locations took us on crazy adventures through crazy parts of the city and even out of town at times. Since this was in the times before cell phones and Mapquest, a Thomas Guide Map was very handy. The directions were so obscure at times, like: "Reset your odometer and then, when you get to 0.8 miles, take a right down the first alley, then go past the abandoned bus and proceed to the 12th warehouse and park, then walk to the left for 50 steps." One time, I even walked through a pasture with cows and horses, tripping balls to get to a party! When you heard the music and felt the bass, you knew you arrived. Finding the party was finding the treasure.

I treasure these memories and always will. There are so many crazy stories and experiences that I will always carry with me. Raving opened dimensions when I was most open. The scene was something to dive into.

The underworld. The underground. Music unlocked the key, and the bass set you free. The experiences I had raving and going to warehouse parties in the '90s changed me as an adolescent and helped me grow into the open-minded adult that I am today. I will forever be grateful for the experiences in the rave scene. Shout out to all the DJs and promoters that made it happen, and especially all the pioneers in the L.A. underground.

6 DJ SINNER - THE SEED ('92)

DJ Sinner is a self-taught DJ/producer from Indio, California.

My name is Jerry Perales, and my artist name is Sinner, a.k.a. DJ Sinner. I'm Mexican-American "Chicano," born in Indio, California. The story that I'm about to share is how my life changed, and how I was saved from being surrounded by the dangers of gang violence, by becoming a party-thrower and an electronic music DJ/Producer.

My family has a strong musical background, ranging from guitarists, keyboardists, drummers, percussionists, violinists, saxophonists, and flautists. When I was between the ages of eight and nine years old, I grew up listening to early electronic techno and hip-hop, from artists such as Afrika Bambaataa, Newcleus, Kraftwerk, Art of Noise, Twilight 22, and Hot Streak, just to name a few.

My older cousins had a DJ setup, and I was always at their house playing records and learning the fundamentals of beat matching. This was back in 1983-1984, when breakdancing was at its popular peak. The movies "Breakin'" and "Beat Street" came out in theaters, and my parents took me and my cousins to see both of them. Of the two, "Beat Street" had a huge influence on me. Halfway through the movie, I knew what I wanted to do with my life, as I had always envisioned myself as some sort of musician. I asked my parents to buy me a DJ setup, but they couldn't afford it at the time. They told me once I graduated from high school, I was to get a job, so that I could buy my own. Right then and there, it became my goal to get my DJ setup and start producing my own electronic music.

Of course, there were many events that happened in my life between being nine years old and graduating from high school. It was not easy growing up in a barrio neighborhood with gang members being my peers. Between fifteen and sixteen, I was hanging with the wrong crowd, one that would have led me to prison or death. All I can say is, "Thank God for the rave culture."

Throughout my teenage years, I had many friends go to jail and prison for gang-related crimes, such as drive-by shootings, drug dealing, etc. Every day was barrio 'hood survival. I also lost three personal friends of mine due to gang violence: Casper, Kenny and Boxer. As a matter of fact, the day that I went to my first rave in the summer of 1992, my father called my uncle's house in San Diego to speak to me. He asked me how I was doing, what I was up to, how my summer vacation was going. I told him that everything was fine and that I was having fun. Then my father asked me the name of my friend that lives across the street catty-corner from us. I told him Adrian (Boxer) and asked my father, "Had he gone to the house looking for me?"

My father paused and asked me if I was sitting down. My blood dropped and I asked if something was wrong. My father told me that Boxer had gotten murdered at a party. A fight had broken out, and a rival gang member pulled out a gun and shot my friend several times. I dropped the phone and cried my heart out. I wanted to go home…I was livid! Then my family came in to see what was wrong, because I was crying hysterically. I just wanted to go home, I was ready to jump on a Greyhound. My cousin grabbed me and told me, "You're not going home. No way. You're staying here with me. I already know what's going through your head. If you go home, you'll be next. You're staying here and you're going to The Seed tonight whether you like it or not."

That day was one of the worst days of my life. I was in a complete daze and my friend was on my mind the whole time. We were very close. Adrian had always looked after me and took care of me. He may have been a notorious gang member, but he was still my true friend. To this day, I miss him dearly.

My cousin was firm that I was going to come out to the party, and that's how I experienced my first rave at the age of sixteen. The rave was held in a roller rink in the city of Chula Vista. This was when there was a phone number that you had to call on the rave flyer to give you directions to a map point.

We called the number on the flyer, then got to the map point, where we were handed another map that led us to another map point. Once we got there, we were given an egg, with instructions indicating to not break or lose the egg or we would not receive the final directions to the rave. We got to the final map point, turned in the egg, and were given the final map with the directions to the actual party.

Once we got to the rave, it was midnight and they weren't letting anyone in. We had to wait in the parking lot for over an hour. This was my first rave and I was still agitated. I was like, "What the fuck? We had to go through all of those map point things to get directions, we're here now, and they won't let us in? What kind of fucking party is this?"

My cousin started talking with me about my life and the direction I was heading. He told me to get my mind off of the situation and that my friend wasn't coming back, and if I were to retaliate in any way when I were to return home, he still wouldn't be coming back. "Don't get caught up; it's not worth it. Your family loves you."

As we were talking, one of my cousin's friends came over to us. He asked what was wrong and my cousin told him what was up. My cousin's friend gave me a hug, then he took out a squared piece of paper and told me to hold it for him, but to hold it in my hand and not to put it in my pocket. Just to close my hand, make a fist and hold the little squared piece of paper. He said, "I'll be right back in 10 minutes. Don't drop the paper, okay?" I said, "Sure"...then when he returned, he said "Let me have it." I opened my hand and the paper was no longer there. It had disintegrated. I asked him if that was some kind of magic trick. He said, "Sort of," then laughed and walked away.

It was about 1:30 AM when they finally decided to open the doors and let people in. All I could hear was the low sub bass rumbling from the inside of the rave, and all I kept saying to myself was, "What am I in for???"

Once we got inside, I felt a sudden change. I began to see things...I was hallucinating. I was in a new dimension where all my troubles were gone. My mind was blown away. I could feel the bass in my chest, and the lights and the psychedelic visuals were amazing. The people at the rave were very friendly. Several of them gave gave me candy, glow sticks, hugs, and everyone was dancing and having a blast. I had the best time of my life. My world of worries no longer existed.

When we left the rave and got in my cousin's truck, the time read 8:00 AM and we just looked at each other and laughed our asses off. He knew I was going to be in big-shit trouble with my mom. When my cousin dropped me off at my uncle's house, he told me to put the blame on him, and then drove away like a bat out of hell. When I got inside, my mom was beyond pissed, and all I told her was, "I'm sorry, but it's my cousin's fault. We went to a party and he didn't want to leave." Then I ran to the back room and locked the door, where I stayed up the whole day. I couldn't sleep—my adrenaline and mind were in overdrive. Oh man, what a phenomenal memory. Being introduced to the rave scene at sixteen was beyond amazing. The people, the culture, the lifestyle, and most importantly the music blew my mind and had given me an unforgettable experience.

The theme of that rave was "The Seed," and a seed was definitely planted in my soul that summer night of '92. From that point onward, I continued to attend raves all over Southern California throughout the '90s and early 2000s. This included parties such as How Sweet It Is, JujuBeats, Narnia, Together as One, Electric Daisy Carnival, and nightclubs that had rave atmosphere such as Attitudes in Riverside, Masterdome in San Bernardino, The Dome at Florentine Gardens Hollywood, Does Your Mama Know on the Sunset Strip, and The Fox Theater in Pomona.

I decided that it was time for me to change my direction in life and no longer hang out with my friends that were involved in gang activity. I tried so hard to talk them, trying to persuade them by having them go with me to a rave. I wanted them to experience what I had experienced, so that maybe they could have fun and leave the gang life. All of them looked at me like I was crazy. They wanted nothing to do with any raves; they were too caught up in their lifestyles. I decided I no longer wanted to hang out with them, and a lot of them were upset at me, because of that. They began to make fun of me by calling me names like Little Raver Boy, Fag, Techno Boy, Techno Sucks…putting me down in any way that they could. But none of it got to me. Those that I thought were my friends were not my true friends at all. The rave culture had enlightened me and brought out the best in me. I was truly blessed and thankful that I had found my calling. It was a gift, and I wanted to somehow, in some way, become more involved with this underground dance culture.

So, I started off promoting underground parties in houses, warehouses and ranches in the early '90s with my new party-crew friends. I saved my money from the parties we threw and I bought my DJ equipment as I had always planned. Wanting to be an electronic music DJ/Producer was a very big challenge for me, because in my entire hometown of Indio, there were no record shops that carried house music, techno, trance, electronic breaks, or drum and bass. As a result, I had to make many trips to the Los Angeles area to buy my vinyl, from shops such as Exodus Records in Rosemead, Tuff Guy Records in Whittier, and, of course, the places on Melrose Avenue: Beat Non Stop, DMC, Street Sounds, and a very groovy shop that was across the street from Beat Non Stop whose name I can't remember, but it was dope. That record shop carried lots of great deep house and cool T-shirts. All of those record shops became my stomping grounds.

Over countless hours of dedication, practice and passion, I managed to create my own style and master my craft. I began to make solid DJ demo mix tapes and was getting DJ gigs, although the gigs that I would get were not what I truly wanted or expected. The crowd would demand hip-hop or old school and didn't offer a lot of room for techno or house music.

Being true to my heart, I went back to promoting for myself, renting clubs and venues that catered to all genres of electronic music. At my clubs and events I would book renowned DJs such as Richard "Humpty" Vission, DJ Irene, Tony B, DJ Larok, Jungle George, Alex Dreamz, and Juan Martinez, to name a few. I wanted my nightclubs and events to be different than what the other clubs had to offer in my hometown. This eventually got me recognized in Indio as "the DJ that only played electronic music."

As I continued to do my nightclub events, I got presented with a radio job in 1998. A local DJ by the name of Emilio the Latin Lover attended one of my nightclub events and offered me the opportunity to host my own underground electronic music show on KKUU 92.7 FM, a new hip-hop and R&B station in Palm Springs. Of course, I took the opportunity and I hosted "The Midnight House Express," which aired from midnight till 2:00 AM. Sadly, there came a time where I was let go from KKUU due to budget cuts, which often happens in radio. I then went to work at another station, KMRJ 99.5 FM, where I got hired as the Production Manager and Imaging Director. I also hosted my own underground electronic music show called "AfterDark with DJ Sinner" on Saturday nights.

As time went on, I continued to DJ throughout Southern California and in 2000, I got into producing for an Anaheim record label named Dynamic Trax International, which was run by the Dynamic Dual, Cesar

G and Jonny Lexxs. I'm proud to say that my days of producing originate in the vinyl days, when I produced my first record entitled "Filter Jazz," which ended up on a 3-track EP called "The Kings of Midi." One track was produced by Tony B!, the second was produced by The Dynamic Dual and the third was produced by yours truly, DJ Sinner.

I have continuously evolved as a producer by producing different styles of electronic music with my producing partner and recording engineer Von Ukuf. Von and I have produced for various labels in the scene, such as Tape Deck Music, Let's Beat Milo Records, C.O.N. Records, Synbot Records, Hardstyle Warriors Recordings, and 5050 Global Muzik. We still work together to this day.

I am truly blessed to have accomplished my DJ/Producer vision that I had as a child, experiencing my first rave at sixteen, falling in love with the '90s underground rave scene, and becoming part of the global electronic music community in such a glorious way that I had never imagined possible. The rave scene saved my life, and helped me become who I am today. God Bless.

7 JUICY JAY ('94)

Juicy Jay is a Los Angeles-based club and rave DJ/promoter, and one of the leaders of the 1990s L.A. Club Kid movement.

I started raving in the early 1990s, when my friends and I graduated from playing Dungeons and Dragons at coffee bars to dancing at undergrounds. They were called underground, because that was slang for you having to know someone who knew someone who was connected enough to get the address of just the map point! Then once at the map point, one would have to look for some random-looking person who you would tell a password to, and who would then take your money and give you the address.

Then my friends and I started throwing outdoor raves called Liberation, at about the same time as another group of friends was doing another outdoor rave called Moontribe. Liberation was an annual event that I would throw with my friends Joseph, Evan, Joe, Eric and Mike, as we extended our ritual camp-out party to the public in 1992-93 up in the mountains, near the San Gabriel River and Angeles Crest Highway. Back then, raves were illegal, and when I first promoted Liberation, there usually were not a lot of people there; small gatherings in the mountains in secret spots.

In 1996, Liberation was pretty amazing. There was a place I came across with my friend Joseph, and we had cut the locks off with bolt cutters to gain access. I had promoted the event with the flyer I had hand-drawn myself. The DJs on the flyer included Hot Wheelz, Jason Splat, Danny Cosmo, Holly Luv Cat, Alien Tom and Demigod. Later that night, up on Lightning Point, I led approximately 1,600 people up a one-way dirt road to a truly majestic destination where we partied all night and watched the sun rise over the city.

Juicy Jay, self-portrait

Besides my own gigs, there were so many raves that I went to—sometimes three or four in one night—but some were just really epic. One of the most outrageous events ever had to be "Xperience" in Palos Verdes, which is in the South Bay area south of Los Angeles. This rave was in a beautiful spot by the ocean in a mansion of sorts, with many rooms, which had separate door nameplates, as if there were a company of some kind behind each door. The mansion had a guest house in the back serving up margaritas. Thomas Michael and Doc Martin were just a couple of the DJs I remember rocking that event when the cops came to the door the first night. Luckily for us, this girl told them that her dad was away and the officers simply told her to keep the noise down.

The party went on for two and a half days after that. Everyone was on psychedelics and booze, mixed with a little E and some nitrous oxide. At some point, I walked through one room like I was Logan from "Logan's Run," in that scene where everyone is in a pile of just people everywhere! People rubbing each other and passing things around. It was a new era of LOVE like we'd read about in the 1960s Flower Power era, but it was our turn to feel it.

On the third day, I felt like we definitely had overstayed our welcome, especially after everyone there had gone skinny dipping in the pool, fucked in all the beds, fucked on all the couches, used the kitchen, the barbecue, the showers, everything. I had the feeling it was time to go, so I had my bag packed and ready to leave. I had to wait for someone who was driving, since there was no Lyft or Uber in those days, but ravers tended to just band together and hang out with other ravers—especially those who had a ride to the party! But as I was waiting, a hard knock rapped at the door. I knew it was the police back this time, but now with dogs! I secretly led ten people out the backyard, over two fences and through an elementary school, before we walked all the way back around to see our fellow ravers sitting in a row in the front yard with handcuffs on. That was our cue to bounce! Had to find an alternate ride back to my home in San Gabriel, but that was just an inconvenience next to being arrested.

I had to have been to at least a hundred raves before I was even eighteen years old, and by the time I turned eighteen, I was one of the main

street promoters of the first big techno club in L.A. called Magic Wednesdays, which was originally run by four people: Jason Jay, Kay Moonstar,
Eli Star, and Auro Michael. After the club started to really take off, Jason
took over the club with his girlfriend at the time, Juliet Long. During the
seven years I promoted for Magic Wednesdays, it went through many
changes, featured hundreds of DJs from all over the world, brought the
NYC Club Kid scene to L.A., and started a fashion revolution in the
process.

The rave scene was always a safe good vibe place to dance and socialize for the most part, and we had to fight for the right to dance, like in
the movie "Footloose," but that was what happened…and then undergrounds became festivals that became more and more corporate. Every
style we created was copied and resold in the shops on Melrose. I was
one of the first L.A. Club Kids, back when our scene was just emerging
in the city. Club Kids were walking, breathing pieces of art, well-known
for hosting parties around the world before there were superstar DJs. A
lot of young celebrities used to attend the clubs and raves I promoted as
well; Mena Suvari used to flirt with me all the time.

Eventually, Juliet and I started our own artsy glam/techno club in
Hollywood called Euro-Trash with Resident DJs Keoki, Daniel Ash (Bau-
haus/Love And Rockets) and myself, with an array of L.A. Club Kids.
By 1999, it felt to me like the true heart of the rave scene was dying. All
my friends and I were becoming 21 years old and could go to all sorts of
nightclubs and were no longer restricted to child-like raves and underage
events. As EDC and other Insomniac brand events got bigger and bigger,
the core of the scene seemed to dwindle.

In 2001, I did an event called Disco Bloodbath, named after the book, located at the Dragonfly in Hollywood. At that time, I was also doing an after-hours in a photography studio in Hollywood, mostly after Club Makeup or Cherry would close. These were places you could go and dress up like a total freak and you wouldn't be the only one…It was marvelous! Very Andy Warhol meets Guns N' Roses. Then I started promoting a place called The Basement, which was an adult underground after-hours in Hollywood that just might go down as one of the most infamous spots

Club Kids in Hollywood. Photo: Michael Tullberg

of all time! The events that I promoted there were called Lick: the Fashionably Kinky Afterhours, where I teamed up with a friend in the scene named Colonel Clique. We used a new portable DJ rig to rock out many parties up until 2004, when the Basement was closed down after an epic New Year's event that was so packed that sweat was dripping off the ceiling!

By 2004, I'd teamed back up with Jason Jay to produce "The Best Event In L.A.," according to the LA Weekly New Year's edition. It was Club Party Monster Volume 1, located at the Avalon in Hollywood, where I brought the Club Kid scene back from the dead. Club Party Monster was hosted by Alexis Arquette (RIP), James St. James, and Rocky Raccoon. Spinning were resident superstar DJ Keoki and Juicy Jay, plus so many DJs that we debuted or brought back. Club Kids united from all over the country and it made it okay for everyone to be a Club Kid once again.

In the following years, Volume 2 would be located at the Vanguard in Hollywood, while Volume 3 was held at the Henry Fonda Theater. Each show featured live bands, DJs and Club Kids galore! After throwing this event in L.A. for three years in a row, Club Party Monster had gotten so popular that other promoters began approaching us to do a replica of my event in their town, so Keoki and I toured the country for five years, DJing together all over, with all kinds of crazy adventures along the way.

But that is another story.

8 SID ZUBER - THE PEOPLE WHO LOVE YOU ('94)

Sid Zuber is an old-school underground Los Angeles rave promoter.

It was November 19, 1994.

"The Doorway to the future is in your mind" were the words placed inside our fortune-cookie invites for the very first "official" party I did, called "Opium," along with a date and voicemail for the recipients to call. To add to the vibe, I did a voice impression on the party's voicemail of a wise old man, sharing what to expect. The vision I had for the party was based on my passion for martial arts, Bruce Lee, and all the action-packed kung fu movies I'd watched over and over while growing up. I was quite fond of fortune cookies and the excitement of opening one, so using this as a promotional tool made a lot of sense to me. Some thought I was crazy for spending significantly more money on these cookies on top of printing a flyer, but it didn't matter to me—it was all about building the hype!

"The People Who Love You!!!" was our promotion group that was born in Los Angeles. We were a collective of friends (Dj Xavier, Markus Manley [R.I.P.], Val and others who came in and out of our lives) who met weekly at raves, wherever the map point led us. They led us to friendships, adventures, my house, and sometimes trouble. We referred to ourselves as "The People Who Love You!!!" as a tribute to anyone and everyone coming together with us for a positive experience. As promoters, we all added our own unique spin on the overall theme, and amazing memories happened as a result. We all wanted the crowd to feel the vibe, from the moment they received a flyer to the overall experience of themed production. It all had to be tied in, and we made sure that it was.

The inspiration for Opium took place while I attended another party called Narnia, and was hanging out in the artist tent with GWAR. Funny how I met them. The festival organizers had a series of tents and vendors on a hillside overlooking the festival grounds in the lower valley. I was walking through the vendor area leading down the hill, when I came across a vendor named Lulu who was a regular at my events. She was a delightful spirit, and always offering free trinkets and free goodies. She placed a colorful necklace around my neck. It was a short black necklace with a black-light hand-painted caterpillar on it. Lulu tried to explain to me the significance of the necklace, but it was quite loud, so I didn't hear the explanation until shortly after. After running into many friends, one of them pulled me into a teepee where a small group of performers were preparing for their set. One of the artists pulled at my necklace and asked if he could use it. I hadn't realized until that point that it had a secret area that unscrewed and served as a pipe.

After that, well…let's put it this way: I know we were sending out smoke signals from the top of the teepee tent, because it was quite cloudy in there for some time. The people in the tent took a liking to me and invited me and my caterpillar to join them, and we all began walking down the path to the festival. As we made our way down, the festival lights dimmed and all the focus was on us coming in. I didn't realize I was a going to be a part of GWAR's live show and it was life-changing for me! It inspired me to have private invite house parties at my house at Venice and Sawtelle Boulevards, just off the 405 freeway.

House parties? Yes, I happened to have four roomies who were from all walks of life. They had no connection to the electronica music I loved, but they were rockers who appreciated a great party. Our house was great for parties, because we had a front door that had a small window near the top of the door, which opened to reveal a pair of eyes. "What's the password?" Just like in the old black-and-white gangster movies.

These parties were often attended by an eclectic group of party people, from ravers to punkers to party crashers. I mean, where else could I see DJ Thee-o spinning house in my living room next to my roommate's piranha tank, while Rob Zombie was hanging talking to my roommate who was a roadie? My roommates loved to party and drink. They soon also became fascinated by rave culture and we all meshed together well. One of my roomies designed punk flyers and was known as "Scum." He had some crazy skills to get everyone he invited to show up. The crazy part about Scum was he didn't drink or do any party favors. If he went through a 2-liter of Pepsi at the party, he was a happy person.

All of us at P.W.L.Y. would invite 20 or so people each, and we always had a good diverse group of about a hundred there. Pasquale from Insomniac often asked me if I was worried about inviting so many people I didn't know into my house. I never did, because I believe there is good in all of us and I was willing to take my chances. Over the course of many house parties, I had two electric razors stolen, and one night, even had a gun pulled on my friends in my bedroom…because the deejay was not spinning Depeche Mode. No one was even hurt, but after that, we always made sure we had at least one DM record on hand and I started to use disposable razors to shave. Clean-up was a group effort, as friends stayed until morning to help clean up and recover from a fantastic night of music and friends. FatBurger was on the catty-corner from us, and their egg sandwiches became our go-to once the sun had risen.

After many successful parties at the house, we decided it was time to try and have an event at a legit venue. I found a place (now called Fantasy Island) near home where an acid jazz club by Marques Wyatt called "Blowfish" was held on occasion. The concept of our first party was based on the poppy flower that generates opium, which is also the state flower of California. We printed a small amount of flyers and a small amount of wrapped fortune cookies with our date, voicemail and a message: "The Doorway to the Future is in your mind," and the rest is history. The overall flyer fit in your pocket and featured a wise man with a classic Fu Manchu mustache who was hovering over a steam pot. The back side of the flyer featured our lineup, mostly of friends. We couldn't afford to make larger flyers with fancy full-color artwork at the time, so we trusted our friends' network, our fortune cookies and a positive vision to help guide us. We themed out the event with yin-yang die-cuts, Chinese lanterns, kabuki-themed Club Kids, and a giant gong that was struck outside as we announced your arrival. Prior to the doors opening, we had a line down the block! It was a great feeling knowing our vision was felt and believed in by over five hundred people.

I was truly inspired by all the love that day in November of 1994, so much so that I ended up producing over eighty P.W.L.Y. events, such as Weeble World, Digital Hut, Psychedelic Circus, Secret Squirrel, Mission To Mars, and Opium. One of my all-time favorite venues is the Glass House in Pomona. This was my home, because I had 100% support of Perry Tollett, who co-ran the place. Perry is an amazing visionary who helped me communicate my crazy ideas to the city. Heck, we shut down city blocks time and time again for Opium and Weebleworld annually, which hit over 4,000 people. This connection led me in 1999 to Paul Tollett and an opportunity to work on the greatest festival on earth...the Coachella Music & Arts Festival. I ended up working on Coachella for thirteen years. Since then, I have designed, produced, toured, and consulted for festivals and corporate client activations.

And to think that it all started with a dream, GWAR, and promotion that you could eat. The world is funny that way sometimes.

Original "Opium" flyer, with info line numbers obscured.

9 DARCEY KEARNEY - I DON'T MISS THE ROAD ('94)

Darcey Kearney is a former rave DJ who lives in Los Angeles.

As a DJ and never really a participant in the rave scene, I may have a different viewpoint from that of the average raver. The scene was never a lifestyle for me. I was all about the music that coursed through my veins. I felt every musical frequency as an emotion. One note or chord can move me to tears or send me into another dimension where time doesn't exist. Music is my therapy and my escape from the harshness the world can bring up on us. However, because I didn't party, I always felt a bit like an outcast in the scene. I think I saw enough of what was happening around me, traveling over 23 years, to keep me far away from the chemicals being taken by many. I remember when crystal meth hit the scene big in 1994, as well as heroin for a few years, which started with people smoking opium. I remember GHB as well: people passing out on the dance floor, one collapsing on one of my turntables while I was playing.

I would put drug-awareness messages on and in my mixed tapes. I had people write to me from prison, saying how those messages got them through some hard times with their addictions. I was no saint, but I was certainly happy that I could try and do my part to be a positive role model in the scene as much as possible.

I have many stories that I can barely recall the details of, but for some reason a trip to Indianapolis (I think?) comes to mind. I was in three or four cities a week for so many years, I'm not sure exactly; it may have been St. Louis. Nonetheless, this trip stood out. It was early in my career, maybe 1993 or 1994. Ernie Munson and I arrived and were picked up at the airport by some sketchy characters that were the promoters' worker bees, in a beat-up car that reeked of cigarettes. I didn't even want to sit on the car seat. The driver then dropped us off at a tweaker crash pad and then left. We had no idea when he was coming back to get us; he just left us there. Even Ernie wasn't really comfortable sitting on that nasty couch. The whole house was full of trash on the floor, garbage bags piled up on the kitchen floor spilling over. The smell in this place was beyond describable!

I walked outside into the backyard through the broken down back door and steps, and the backyard was full of trash as well. I was sooooooo uncomfortable here. I mentioned to Ernie that I packed incense. We burned all of it. Then someone who was either living or crashing there entered the living room and barely even acknowledged us. He sat in a broken-down rocking lounge chair that was permanently tilted forward and looked incredibly uncomfortable. The kid sat there hunched over, obsessively playing video games. He was two feet away from us and it was like we weren't even there. He never said hi or even looked at us. It was so strange. We felt invisible, for he was right in front of us.

It had been a couple of hours that we'd been in this place, and it was getting dark. I was dying to get out of there—where was the promoter to take us to our hotel to get ready for the show? But from what I recall, we had to get ready at this house and we were taken directly to the event from there. We had to eat drive-through fast food on the way to the event (not my normal kind of meal). It was just awful, so awful that I can't even tell you about the party, because it obviously didn't stand out as much as the tweaker crash pad we were left at. After the event, from what I can remember, we had to stay at the venue until the end and then head straight to the airport. I guess that is one way to get out of paying for a hotel for you DJs. Oh, I don't miss the early days of traveling for gigs before I had contracts in place.

My next most memorable, as would be for any DJ, is when my records were lost by American Airlines. I had just played at Simon's in Ft. Lauderdale, I think it was. There was a storm when we were flying home, which meant our plane had to land in Key West, where I spent the night on the airport floor until we could fly out in the morning. When I finally arrived back at home in San Francisco, my records didn't show up. I never saw them again. I had all my 1950s sound-effects records and my treasured Willy Wonka 12" with a sample I used in my Androidgeny mix tape. To make things worse, I was also due to leave in three days for Germany for a two-month tour, where I played a rave event in Stuttgart (I think) with Armand Van Helden, who played every version of his 1994 big hit, "The Witch Doctor," back-to-back for about an hour of his 90-minute set.

Anyway…when I arrived in Frankfurt, Andy Horvath (who I was touring with) took me directly to a record outlet. It was amazing and overwhelming all at once. I got some great music straight from a distribution warehouse in Germany...I was stoked on that tip, needless to say. But even with all the new amazing music I just got, I wasn't familiar with it and BAM, we were on tour. I just had to make it happen, and it made for a long, uncomfortable two months, which included getting sick from some bad fish in Poland and being violently ill in front of TV and radio crews at the house we were all staying in. That was, by far, my most humiliating experience EVER. I also never got my tour of Auschwitz while over there because of that. The locals said I would have been just as sick going there.

Through that tour, there was a lot of staying in people's homes as well as hotels in between the nights of the gigs. There was a lot of humility in washing your underclothes in people's bathroom sinks and hanging your stuff out to dry. Mind you, I was the only girl traveling with the group on this tour. Zero privacy or alone time. Guys teasing you or hitting on you nonstop and partying, which I didn't do much of. It was exhausting, but it was all worth it in the end. Memories and relationships were made with many people, and language barriers were crossed through the pulse of the music, our common language. It was all an experience I now cherish and will never forget. Thank you Andy Slate (who now lives here in So Cal, many years after this tour!) for bringing me to Germany for such a grand tour of your homelands, Germany and Hungary.

I'm also grateful for all my travels—local, through Canada, and overseas. I wouldn't trade it for anything, although maybe now I have. I'm now a dog trainer with a successful dog-walking business in L.A. Who'd have thought? Those who know my animal past get it, though, for music and animals have always been my two passions. It was just time for change and to get connected with the earth, being outside with the dogs all day and helping rescue dogs and their owners understand each other. I can definitely say I've lived a few lives, and I'm so grateful for all the experiences!

Photo: Michael Tullberg

10 HOUMAN SALEM - LOGIC ('94)

Houman Salem is the founder of ARGYLEHaus of Apparel, a successful fashion design and manufacturing company.

The early 1990s were a strange but exciting time to be in the L.A. music scene. For me, it all started at a club called Logic in Santa Monica. My friend, Christine, discovered this place and insisted that I go with her the next time she went. She went on and on about how amazing it was: "You're not going to believe it...the music, the vibe, the people!" The only problem was that Logic opened its doors at midnight on Sundays. I thought she was crazy. Who in their right mind was going to show up anywhere at midnight, and on a Sunday? It didn't take much convincing, though; at that time, I had just graduated college and was working in the Publicity department at Capitol Records in Hollywood. I didn't know what to expect, but I thought maybe I would discover something interesting and make a name for myself in the company.

Logic was a small, hole-in-the-wall club with a capacity of maybe 100 people, and when we showed up a little before midnight, there was a crowd of like 500 people trying to get in. Christine was already a regular there, so we walked right in, and from that point, my life changed forever. You have to remember, we were in the post-Nirvana era of rock and roll and every club in L.A. was booking grunge bands. Every record executive was wearing flannel and scouting for the next big thing in grunge…but this was something completely different. It was one guy up on stage with turntables, making the most amazing sounds I'd ever heard. This was the birth of House music on the West Coast, and the DJ was a British guy named Mark Lewis. Christine had become friends with Mark weeks earlier, and she introduced us at the end of that night.

Mark and I hit it off immediately. His knowledge of music was deep, and not just House music. We could easily discuss Pink Floyd, The Smiths and Soundgarden, then argue over which recording was better: "Pet Sounds" or "Abbey Road." He was a big-idea type of person (much like myself) and he was out to do something different in the L.A. music landscape. I was drawn into that energy, but it was those Sunday nights at Logic that I looked forward to all week. Soon, you would start seeing the cast of regulars at the club; there was a culture brewing that brought so many unique people together.

I was at Logic just about every week for the next six months. One week after another, Mark would bring over one of his DJ friends from the UK to perform at Logic; struggling young DJs that no one in the States had ever heard of before, trying to break big in America. I was one of the lucky ones to see the likes of Carl Cox, Sasha & Digweed, and Paul Oakenfold perform in those early days at Logic.

In general, the club scene in L.A. was strong in those days, at least in terms of numbers. People went out to have a good time, but the music was becoming somewhat stale. Clubs like The Roxbury, The Century Club, The Gate, and Tempest were always packed, but I don't think most people went for the music. People went out just to go out and the music was always the same mix of hip-hop and disco. Every club would play the same mix. You would hear 2Pac's "California Love" and Gloria Gaynor's "I Will Survive" at least 3 times each night. But Logic was different. Not only was this new music that none of the other clubs would dare to play, it was also a gathering of some of the most unique people in L.A. These were the early adopters of House music. The club itself was a bit of a dive, but no one seemed to care much about their surroundings; the music overpowered the ambiance (or lack thereof). You would see sawdust on the floors and 10-year-old bar stools that were far past their usefulness, but no one cared. We were there for the music.

Those DJs knew exactly how to tap into people's emotions with the use of rhythm and melody. They would calm the crowd down with a slow but steady beat, layered with a soft but repetitive melody that would soothe your soul. They would sustain this moment for several minutes. Everyone would move to the slow beats as if in a trance. Then the DJ would start to build up the beat, add new melodies, pump up the BPMs, elevate the moment to a climate of pulsating rhythms that would make the crowd explode into the euphoric madness of dance.

Over time, Mark and I built a small circle of industry friends, all trying to make a name for ourselves in the music scene. Many of them were DJs, but some of us were aspiring producers, promoters, managers or agents. We would gather at a restaurant in Hollywood called Louis XIV on La Brea and strategize. This was our headquarters back then (and they liked to play House music there). We would ask ourselves, "How can we break this scene big? Who's going to pave the way for House to take shape in this town? How can we get the people to listen?" Everything would eventually fall into place, but we had to wait out the grunge scene first. That was a force too huge to disrupt at that time. This little circle of friends (Carl Cox, Christopher Lawrence, Grant Plant, among others) would eventually become some of the biggest names in the Global EDM industry, but at that point in time, our biggest question at the end of each night was "Who's paying for this bill?"

Those early days of the House music scene in L.A. were truly unique and the scene eventually exploded into a worldwide phenomenon. But I really treasure those early days where a bunch of young ambitious kids set out to change the world. I stayed in the music business for several years, working at a variety of different record labels (Capitol Records, Sony Music Entertainment, MCA/Universal), but I left the industry completely in 2002. After the Napster disruption, people didn't want to pay for music and global record sales began their downward slide. I eventually found my way into the fashion industry where I currently work, but I always tell people that "Music is my one true love; fashion is my mistress."

11 WADE HAMPTON - MILLENNIUM ('94)

Wade Hampton is one of the longest-running and most respected old-school rave promoters and DJs in America. From the Starck Club to the Super Bowl, Wade truly has done it all.

The corner of 5th and Flower. Downtown Los Angeles.

If the end of the world were to take place on New Year's Eve of 1999, I suppose this is about as central a location for Armageddon as you could get. Before the sun had even gone down, the lines between event security and the U.S. military were drawing increasingly blurry. If we had only been more honest with ourselves about the writing on the wall in the years preceding, I suppose it would have made more sense that this is the way it would all go down.

Sunset bounced off the hills far in the distance, where an underground revolution was poking its head up through a manhole somewhere in Hollywood. Knowing what we now know about both the illustrious career of director James Cameron as well as the billion-dollar dance-music industry, it's probably the case that some industry folks will claim this is the moment we truly "arrived."

Well, it was actually only September 17, 1994, as filmmakers set out to create the closing scenes of the Cameron-produced "Strange Days," a film about an ex-cop who is tortured by a collection of data-discs containing memories of crimes. After seeing the completed film later on, it was easier to understand the elusive "Blade Runner" mark that the filmmakers had in mind, but on this evening, there were few details for guests at the film shoot to work with.

The basics: pay $10 to be an extra in a New Year's Eve party scene for this film, featuring Dee-Lite and Aphex Twin, who were on the bill. The venue would be one of the more prominent busy intersections in all of downtown L.A., sitting at the base of the landmark Bonaventure Hotel. This hotel was well-known as a location for many feature films, the most famous probably being "In the Line of Fire," a drama in which John Malkovich meets his eventual demise falling through levels of broken glass to his death. Cameron's movie would also conclude with a scene set in this location. That's pretty much where any similarities between the two films would end.

The notion that an event of this size and scope could become sorta matter-of-fact says a lot about the state of our art at the time. It truly captured one of the most important, yet somewhat fading, hallmarks of the L.A. rave genesis – the undeniable sense of one-upmanship that drove the most innovative thinkers of the time. What set this night apart, though, was that the penchant for grandiose, big ideas for parties had finally become the norm, as if the genie had been put back in the bottle so damn successfully that ravers had come to expect nothing short of the most fantastic possibilities coming to fruition, week in and week out. That emotion of paying to be able to say, "I can't believe what is going on around me right now," was the golden egg we were all looking for. If Circa '92 had whisked L.A. into the computer age, this party, Millennium, was here to lay claim to showbiz turf in the entertainment capital of the world.

At the forefront was a critical early electronic impresario named Philip Blaine, now a critical player at the Coachella festival. Often overlooked amongst the pantheon of early L.A. electronic show producers, he was actually one of the most effective there ever was. Back then, if you had to talk to an L.A. City official during the course of putting on a large-scale dance event, you wanted Phil involved in the conversation. If there were a fire marshal that required an intelligent street-level mediator's touch, you would be wise to involve Mr. Blaine. If you wanted a better promoter deal with a Hollywood club owner - better call Phil. So when James Cameron and director Katherine Bigelow decided they needed more than just a rock band to sustain the crowd into the wee hours for such an elaborate Holly-wood blockbuster scene, they were indeed wise enough to get Philip Blaine on the case. He had enlisted our crew, CPU101, to assist with the street promotion in order to get the 7,000-10,000 people necessary to make it as believable as a mildly apocalyptic, near-future rave scene could be.

Earlier that day, I had received a call from my friend David Prince, one of three creators of the Midwest's lawless, yet most unstoppable, Furthur Festival, which had premiered earlier that year with Aphex Twin headlining. I had been arrested after performing at the end of the 3-day festival and had not seen David since the moments after bailing myself and others out of jail. He wanted to know if it was cool if he and Timothy Leary stopped by the downtown L.A. soiree that evening, as the proposition of such a spectacle had caught the attention of our aging-yet-rowdy LSD guru.

After meeting the two at a prearranged artist entrance backstage, we marveled at the spectacle before us. We were beyond excited to hear Tim proudly proclaim the scene to be the manifestation of ages of modernists that led up to this day. Endless successions of artists, auteurs, minstrels and vagabonds linked together for thousands of years with only one purpose in mind — questioning authority. As we stood backstage talking about destiny, I noticed that there was a flight case onstage stacked on top of a DJ turntable with no lid, literally resting on the tonearm. As we stood there talking, it bugged me more and more until my OCD got the best of me. I finally excused myself to go talk to the sound company so they could better understand how they were about to destroy a $500 turntable.

After removing the case, freeing up the Technics 1200 from certain demise, I turned to the side-stage steps, where my path was suddenly blocked by a short-dreaded man who I believed to be Dee-Lite's tour manager.

He then said, "Hey kid, get me a beer."

Not opposed to being perceived as a kid, but also not wild about his tone, I stepped aside to go around him, simply stating, "Wrong kid."

He steps in front, blocking my path. "I said get me a beer, kid."

Sizing up the beef and the 5-inch height difference, I repeated, "Wrong kid." As he put his hand up to my chest, I added, "Go fuck yourself."

And that was it. With not so much as the blink of an eye, the shorter, seasoned stage manager saw the opportunity and took it. With my back to the edge of the stage and no guardrail to break my fall, a simple push to my off-balanced chest was all it took to launch me off the side and flat on my back on the asphalt below. As the shock of what had just happened set in, and with my head still stinging from bouncing off the concrete, I could see Prince and Leary upside down as I looked up, dazed from the ground below. There was a brief moment where I did stop to consider that I may, in fact, be dead.

As I was helped to my feet, I could see the tiny man hovering from above on the stage laughing, "You ready to get me a beer yet?"

And then, humiliated in front of my mentor and peers, it hit me. Primal instincts kicked in. As I looked at the trash can full of freshly iced beer bottles on the ground beside me, a switch flipped. All in one fluid motion, I grabbed a full beer from the top of the ice and delivered a Nolan Ryan-sized fastball square under the manager's jaw. Still a bit surprised at the accuracy and power of the shot, I can still feel that sound down to my own bones to this day. Not to anyone's surprise, the next few minutes featured a level of drama that only LAPD could dream up, as I was wrestled to the ground in a way that would make my old schoolmate and would-be presidential assassin John Hinckley look like he was getting a nice massage. Apparently shoving someone off a short building is no big deal, but weaponizing a full bottle of Heineken in retaliation for such a transgression is a big no-no. Before Dave whisked him off to safety and he left the chaotic scene, I remember hearing Tim say, "Please don't fight these cops Wade. Relax." Dave reinforcing, "Got you, buddy; don't worry - I'll bail you out in an hour or so."

I was finally lifted to my feet, and the walk of shame to the front door began. Passing by friends and fans, I was hauled in handcuffs by a group of officers to the front gates, with the lines between acting and real life on this movie set becoming harder to discern by the minute. We passed by

my then only-casual-acquaintance Stephanie Smiley, the person in charge
of the revered guest list that night, and who would also eventually mother
my child a couple years later. She offered only silent, air-whispered advice,
mouthing the words, "Shut the fuck up."

Having heard the commotion on event security radios, both my
CPU101 partner Tef Foo as well as Philip Blaine had gone to the front
door to assess the issue, obviously quite surprised and concerned that the
violent on-stage disturbance that had occurred before the doors had even
opened actually involved a partner. This time, it would be Philip cutting
off the path of the police, something I will never forget as long as I live.
Boldly and quite confidently springing into action, Tef arrived by his side
only seconds later. Negotiations were had. Pleading occurred. Promises
were made.

After convincing the officers that this was more of a case of self-
defense than they previously thought, a compromise was eventually struck:
"We won't arrest him, but he has to leave the party." Disappointed but
relieved not to be headed to jail, I almost told Tef to shut up when he
continued to negotiate.

Tef: "How far does he have to leave?"

Officer: "Seriously? He has to leave the party. What part do you not
understand?! We've got our hands full tonight, in case you haven't noticed.
I don't want to see his face here again. Understand?"

Philip: "What if he goes to a room at the hotel that we're working out
of? You won't hear a peep again."

Tef pulls a stack of a dozen room keys out of his pocket, ready to seal
the deal, as the officer contemplates.

Officer: "You realize if we see him again, that's it. And this time, we're laying it on thick. Assault with a weapon. The whole nine. We're going to walk him up to the room, but that's the last I want to see of you tonight. I'm serious."

Tef (fumbling with the keys, handing the officer one in an envelope): "I have no idea who ended up taking which room, because we have the whole floor and I've been down here all day…but here ya go. Big suite too dude - #2231. I'll come hang with you in a while."

Nothing quite like riding the myriad of escalators during a rave at the Bonaventure Hotel wearing a Fresh Jive outfit from head-to-toe…and a pair of handcuffs. I played it cool, leaning against the escalator rail, trying to act as if I weren't headed to a hotel suite with a bunch of plainclothes Los Angeles police officers.

As the officer awkwardly slid the key into the hotel room door, I remember thinking that he seemed unfamiliar with the process. As this fancy security feature was somewhat new, he didn't seem to quite understand that you had to wait for the light, etc. So when the door suddenly burst open, slamming into a dead bolt and making a huge noise after opening only a few inches, everyone in the hotel hallway was startled. I remember a brief silence as all assessed the situation.

If the eyes peeking through the crack between the wall and door were not completely recognizable, the voice that bellowed through the small opening certainly was. My heart sank.

Voice: "Hey guys!"

Officer: "Mind opening the door, please?"

The eyes through the door shift from the police officer to me, with a sweet look masking only 99% of the shock and confusion. Back to the police officers. Then back to me. Smile. Then back to the officers again.

Voice: "Sssurrrre."

After briefly closing to make way for the deadbolt, the door eventually swings open to reveal a fairly solid, scruffy, blond-haired white guy in his late 20s, wearing nothing but a pair of creased Dickies khakis and white Adidas Stan Smiths. No shirt. A bit wild-eyed. Behind him, there is a young man, looking like a model who is clearly now pacing. As we enter the foyer, a massive 3-room hotel suite is revealed. It has panoramic windows spanning the entire length of the room, with downtown L.A. filling up most of the frame.

As the officer begins to unlock the handcuffs, he announces, "Gentlemen. I've brought you a friend for the evening. And he's not to leave this room or he's putting these cuffs back on." Turning to me, they ask, "Are you going to be able to handle this?" Simply dying for the officers to leave the room before they realize that now would be the perfect time to ask everyone in the room for some ID, I humbly reply, "Yes, sir."

As the door closed behind the last officer walking out, I could only think, "If they'd just thrown a net over this room, that entire L.A. rave scene below would lose one of its most critical instigators." Shut up.

Turning to the hoods in the room, I apologized. "Dude. So sorry.... had no idea you two were here."

The same guy, who had once jumped out of a second-story window at the Beverly Hills Hotel to evade the Feds closing in on him, says, "Whatever. It's OK, man. I wish I had the time to stress about those fools rounding you up, but when I tell you what's really gone down over the past 24 hours, you'll understand. This is nothing. Zilch. Nada." Leaning back, now cupping his hands behind his head, he continued, "I do believe we've gotten ourselves in a bit of a rave pickle." Sitting beside him on a couch, I attempted to digest the enormity of what he was saying, and the potential for affordable chaos on the highest level set in. My mind began whirling through the endless possible criminal activities he was describing. He continues, "So kick back; relax, bro. Make a cocktail. You're free. And I think you'll agree with me when I give you the lowdown. Because once again - YOU are nowhere near their biggest problem right now."

Smiling now, he says, "But I know who is."

One day soon, I will tell you the rest of this story.

Wade Hampton and Tef Foo, 2017. Photo: Michael Tullberg

12 KIMBERLY ST. JOHN ('94)

Kimberly St. John is a nurse, DJ, and founding member of Electronic Music Alliance.

The word "rave" was always more of a verb than a noun to me. It meant dancing, feeling, listening, loving, finding, losing, living. The term "EDM" did not exist until very recently on my timeline. To choose one defining story in my days of the rave is nearly impossible, as there are years of stories that have woven in and out of my life, shaping my journey of electronic music.

I must begin at the beginning by recounting those very first raves I attended in the early 90s, with a silver whistle hanging from my neck and baggy jeans sagging off my butt. These raves were in lower downtown Denver, Colorado, in old abandoned warehouses. You only knew about them if you were personally invited, and you didn't know where they were located until you were given a physical paper map of where the secret meeting point was that night. It was all on the down low, nothing like the social media frenzy of today. Anyway, at that meeting point, you followed all the weirdos to…THE RAVE…A DJ named Hipp-E was the first I remember. He was blowing my mind with the music. I don't recall exactly what he was playing, but I do remember hearing lots of Moby's first album (self-titled Moby) around that time. It was released in 1992 and I can still hear the tracks "Go" and "Next is the E" clearly in my mind. Orange Sunshine had a way of making certain tracks sound like a thousand angels singing…but I digress. Green Velvet is another producer I remember hearing lots from back then. And then there was Art of Noise. Wow. And that track "Future

The author, on the dance floor. Photo: Michael Tullberg

Sound of London" by Papua New Guinea. Man, oh man.

Okay, here is one of oh-so-many stories: Cut to years later when I lived in Los Angeles. It's now the late 90s, and I find myself somehow sucked back into the electronic music world. How the hell did that happen? Once a raver always a raver. I'm working (let's be honest, I'm getting paid to party) for Offworld Music, a record label. The office was on a prime spot on Sunset Boulevard in Hollywood. I'm traveling with the Digital Assassins, hanging out with the Crystal Method, BT, and other burgeoning electronic music artists. We're all riding the wave of this genre that is finally catching on in America.

One of my favorite nights was New Year's Eve 2000. What a way to bring in the new millennium! Digital Assassins headlined at Utopia, which was a legendary nightclub in Las Vegas. Fire Mike performed, blowing huge flames from his mouth that you could actually feel from anywhere in the club. Frank Richards played outside on the infamous patio until the sun came up. Everyone danced in sync; no words needed to be spoken. We were all smiling at each other, knowing we were in the midst of something indescribable to anyone else. The massive desert sky overhead glowed pink amber. Inside, a giant champagne fountain flowed, as thousands of people cheered and danced their way into the new century.

I knew I always wanted to go big on every New Year's Eve after this night. The way I saw everyone come together in celebration made me realize that we were on the verge of something really big. Dance music was in full force and was here to stay, making its way into our culture through movies, car commercials, and clubs. To me, dance music is so much more than just music. It's celebrating life to the fullest.

I went to the very first Coachella. As I did cartwheels through the grassy openness, I thought, "Oh, this is going to be GOOD. Goldenvoice is really onto something here." I predicted it would continue as a yearly event and that it would grow bigger each year. No more cartwheels through open land, but I am happy it has grown so big. Offworld Music had a booth set up there and I played some records, so I guess you could say I DJd at Coachella—haha. But I had to pee during my "set," and when I came back, my record bag had been stolen. But it was okay, I just did more cartwheels in the grass.

Miami deserves a story as well. The Winter Music Conference was once oh-so-intimate. Only those in the music industry were going, playing, and partying there. It wasn't exactly open to the public like it is now. It was a place where those of us working in the electronic music industry would meet up in one place annually. One year, I saw Hipp-E play, yes, the DJ I mentioned earlier, the DJ I remember seeing play at my first early 90s rave. I got to tell him that. He was so happy to hear it.

And that's what the rave is all about. Those circles. The beautiful circles that form and come back around in the dance music scene. The connections with others who love to celebrate life as much as you do. It's like nothing else. It's magical.

13 CYRIL PALACIOS - FREQUENCIES ('95)

Cyril Palacios is an electronic music engineer, producer, writer, performer and spokesman.

It was late in the summer of 1995, a dark time for me. I was struggling with many issues in my life: emotional, physical, and also my identity as a musician. Not that I had any talent or been gifted with physical musical abilities; to this day, I always tell my music clients, "I play music with computers as I played as a kid with my Legos - building with little colored blocks." I was alone in Hollywood after the breakup of my band Fear No Art. We'd been dubbed "The Beatles of the '90s" (which we clearly weren't) by our manager Marty Jay, a former New York child star who'd been friends with Andy Warhol's Factory crew in the late '70s. Marty was also a friend of Robert Margouleff, the legendary music producer/engineer/analog synthesist for Stevie Wonder's early 1970s' classic period albums, and the year before, Marty had convinced Robert to invite us to the famous Record Plant studios in Hollywood to play our demo.

When I walked into the studio with my Commodore 128, a Mirage sampler and a Korg M1, Robert said to me, "What is a computer doing in

a music studio? Computers have no business being in a music studio!" It
was Robert's first encounter with potential computer music, and years later
at the Audio Engineering Society dinner keynote, I quoted him saying that
when I first met him (to great laughs). Despite this inauspicious beginning,
Robert would teach me everything I know today about sound, starting
with the book "On The Sensations Of Tone" by Hermann Helmholtz,
which is one of the world's greatest scientific book classics. It bridges the
gap between the natural sciences and music theory.

Unfortunately, even with Robert's help, the band was on its way out.
We got as far as playing one of our songs on an indie commercial radio station in Los Angeles, the groundbreaking MARS FM 103.1. They actually
used my voice in their radio stinger spots between commercials. The singer
of our band was Marty's son, Jason Jay, who, after the group split, began
promoting nightclubs and venues. After the band broke up, I had no real
desire to even think about making music or working with another band.

That summer of '95, I met Jason again at Louis XIV on La Brea Av-
enue on a Monday night. He told me about a new venture of his involving
Auro Michael, DJ Eli Star and Kay Moonstar: a new small club named
Magic Wednesdays. The club was to start at the iconic L.A. nightspot Carlos 'n Charlie's on the Sunset Strip, which would later become Dublin's.
When I got there on their opening night around 11:00, I saw a scene I was
not familiar with at all. Most L.A. clubs in the '90s, such as Bar One, Sin-
A-Matic, Club Cherry, and Michelle's XXX at 7969 were playing mostly
Top 40 music, and maybe some industrial music like Front 242, Prodigy
or Ministry, but that was as edgy as it got – still mainstream KROQ-type
music. The new club Magic Wednesdays wasn't going for that, at all. It

featured Eli Star as the headliner and the opening DJ was Jimmy – neither of whom I'd heard of before in my life.

There is a famous song by Indeep called "Last Night a DJ Saved My Life". Well, it may sound like a cliché, but that was the case here.

When I walked in, Jason greeted me at the door and gave me a wristband and drink tickets. I remember the place as if it were yesterday: it was a low-ceilinged, upstairs, attic-like room, with wisps of smoke billowing from a tiny smoke machine that went off every now and then next to the DJ booth. They had a nice, decent dance floor that was packed and a bit stuffy, because of all the heat rising like an oven from everyone dancing and thumping on the wooden floors. The sound system was tight, solid and had perfect bass. The people were dancing oddly, facing the speakers and the DJ. It was the first time I saw glow-sticks, and what they now call candy ravers: young people wearing oversized clothes with neon colors and lights. It was something new for me, but the biggest surprise was yet to come, when Eli Star played a record that changed my life forever.

The music stopped abruptly and a breakbeat loop started the next track coming up, an ominous "one note" or "single tone" synthesizer acid-line that took over the beat. Out of nowhere came a time-stretched sample of a female voice saying "higher state of consciousness" in a jagged, metallic moan. The acid line was triggered by a Roland TB-303 Bass Line synthesizer, an obscure analog synth released in 1982 that has a single audio oscillator, which produces either a saw-tooth wave or a square wave.

There was no "harmony," there was no "melody," there wasn't even a conventional music arrangement in the sense of verses, chorus, bridge, etc. The song's emotion was derived solely from the "frequencies" from the

TB-303, piercing highs and lows. This was a musical shockwave and was revolutionary on many levels: it defied conventional wisdom concerning "tonality" and "harmonic justice"—meaning, here they have people dancing and having a spiritual experience with no words and no music at all really; just frequencies. The record was "Higher State of Consciousness" by American DJ Josh Wink, first released in March 1995.

This new sound had nothing to do with music in the sense that a symphonic arrangement would, if you will. Yet in its "monotony," it delivered a mystical approach to sound, expanding the aural universe with microtonality within psychoacoustics. I went home and began making sound experiments with my computer, emulator sampler and synths - trying to recreate the amazing experience I had heard at Magic Wednesdays. That experience brought me to a new way of looking at music and sound in general. I felt hope for my abilities, being nearly tone-deaf, as my elementary music teacher so eloquently put it. I quickly put a dance track together with just an acid-line envelope, and I was amazed at how much freedom there is in electronic music when you escape the chromatic scale in western sound formats; freedom is the essence of sound itself.

From that day on, I began the journey of experimenting with "frequencies," rather than focusing on tonality. Remember, at this time, we were still years away from the Internet, PCs or Macs having the performance we know today. However, human desire for innovation and competition would rapidly advance the field towards faster microprocessors - crunching prime numbers from algorithms, soon creating the software/hardware leapfrog battle we continue having to this day.

At first, the best thing a computer could do with sound was sampling—just playing back or triggering a recorded sound file. But soon, I acquired the new Atari 1040ST with Cubase 1.0, the first home computer with MIDI ports. Atari and Steinberg created the market for products we now know as "Home Studio" for consumers – stuff that you and I could buy and bring home. The Atari 1040 STF with Cubase was capable of recording CD-quality sound on a hard disk up to 6 minutes in stereo, which was pretty hefty back then. The Internet, as we know it today, was not around yet, but through phone calls and places like Nadine's Music in Hollywood, I made contact with the Cubase sales representatives from Germany. Our relationship became about software and hardware issues from a "consumer" standpoint, basically me doing unofficial research and development for the programmers.

As fate would have it, "frequencies" would change my life again, as I put together another electronic music band and demo in 1996 with Jason Jay; we named ourselves "Swirl." At that point, Jason was at the peak of his Magic Wednesdays success, knew everyone in the Los Angeles club scene, and every artist. Being a great promoter, he set up a meeting with Steve Levy from Moonshine Records, which was a tiny L.A.-based indie electronic music record label doing business out of the Taft Building on Hollywood and Vine, and then later at their headquarters in West Hollywood. Steve said to meet him at the Winter Music Conference in Miami in March. The name "Winter Music Conference" in the middle of Spring Break in Miami made no sense to me, but I went because I knew people from the new DJ music scene and software scene would be there.

During the conference, I spoke at a music panel. After the audience Q&A, I was approached by Ines Garstecky, the marketing director for

Magix Entertainment, a German software company and authors of Samplitude, which was a small consumer-based Windows audio and video application. I never managed to meet up with Steve Levy, but when I got back home to L.A., I met again with Ines at the Magix Entertainment U.S. office. Ines proceeded to show me the new Magix Music Maker and Music Studio software, running out of a Dell PC Laptop with the latest Intel processor inside (I think that later became their slogan "Intel inside"), and I was blown away! With my years of experience working with Cubase, it was very easy for me to use its programs, and we pushed the envelope testing Intel chips' processing power on Dell laptops. Music Maker ended up being the first consumer-based "audio and video" Windows software.

During that meeting with Ines, I reproduced Josh Wink's sound on their "analog simulator synth software," and they were amazed at what I did in a minute, seemingly effortlessly composing modern music. That's what they had been looking for in Miami: someone to show the world their product. Ines quickly asked me if I'd be interested in going on a North American tour promoting their new software with the UK's Ninja Tunes record label. Of course, I said yes.

The tour headliners were Cold-Cut and Kid Koala. We played everywhere, in all major venues in every major city in North America. I was now hooked on electronic music and its possibilities for my life and career. Meanwhile, as technology continued to advance rapidly, I got the chance to work with one of the most amazing pioneering talents in electronic music. It was again at Magic Wednesdays, where Jason introduced me to the main DJ that night: Superstar DJ Keoki, who would draw me further into the epicenter of the electronic music scene. Keoki was the first DJ ever in history to sell one million records. He was renting the back club area of the same venue as Magic Wednesdays, the World Club at 7070 Hollywood Boulevard. Keoki invited me to come to his place for after-hours drinks and to play some music. Jason insisted I play Keoki our "Swirl" demo, and when Keoki heard my writing and production skills, he hired me on the spot to work with him on his next project. A few weeks later, I was hired by Moonshine Records to co-write Keoki's album "Jealousy" for the next two years (that experience is another book altogether). The record was later remixed by Grammy-award-winning dance music producer Dave Aude, and this became Moonshine Records official release of "Jealousy."

After Keoki's album was finally finished, I reconnected again with Robert Margouleff who, by this time, was working on the new HD audio technology during the bitter home-theater battle between HD DVD and Blu-Ray, which Blu-Ray won. Nevertheless, HD audio brought me to the next level of "frequency," which was multichannel surround-sound technology. When Robert saw what I was doing with the Dell laptop and Magix software, he set up a meeting at Digital Theater Systems (DTS). I met with the CEO, Jon Kirchner, and legendary musician Rory Kaplan, who both agreed that I should be hired under an NDA (Non-Disclosure Agreement) to pilot a project for DTS at the legendary Ministry of Sound in London. At Ministry, I performed the first-ever HD surround-sound DJ club mix, using Dell laptops and Germany's Samplitude 6.1. It was the first time anyone ever saw audio/video coming out of a laptop in a place like MOS. In the year 2000, PCs were it, while Macs (Apple) were light years away - still trying to make IBM processors compete with Intel (they failed)

For the next two years, I travelled as an evangelist of Surround Sound, working again with Robert Margouleff who, along with his engineering partner, Brant Biles, became the pioneers of "nearfield mixing". This was a new mastering technique for "non-theatrical" performances such as home entertainment (video games, Blu-Ray, TV, cable, streaming audio), destination venues (planetariums, concert halls), and dance clubs. By 2004, the nearfield mix industry was in full swing as home theaters with surround-sound audio exploded in global markets. Robert and Brant opened Mi Casa Multimedia, a boutique audio post house specializing in forensic audio restoration and HD audio. At the height of Mi Casa's production output, it included the entire New Line Cinema catalogue as well as the "Lord of The Rings" extended trilogy for Peter Jackson.

During my five years at Mi Casa as new business development VP and manager, I acquired extensive knowledge about multichannel audio presentation in venues of various sizes, but nothing would prepare me for what was to come next: the most significant part of my journey in "frequency" yet. During Spring Break of 2007, we took a break from post-production on "The Lord of the Rings" trilogy to go to WMC. The post supervisor from New Line, Jesse Torres, was working on the WMC visuals with Vello Virkhaus from V2 Labs in L.A. who, at the time, was dating my dear friend from Magic Wednesdays, DJ Sandra Collins. Small world! I had spoken in technology panels before at WMC in Miami and I knew Sandra from the Keoki warehouse days in L.A. – this was a no-brainer; we were going to Miami. That WMC turned out to be legendary.

We arrived in South Beach and ended up staying at the Victor Hotel on Ocean Avenue. It was a hot spring morning and on the upstairs patio, there were about ten people having espresso martinis, while Tiesto casu-

*Jesse Torres, Vello Verkhaus, DJ Sandra Collins and Cyril
Palacios at the Victor Hotel in Miami. Note Tiesto playing in
the background. Photo unknown.*

ally played in the corner, all by himself, practicing his DJ set for Ultra
Music Festival the next day. Next thing we knew, we were invited to go up
to Prodigy's suite at the hotel. I said *"What?"* I was blown away, because
I've been a huge Prodigy fan since their record, "Charlie", was released
way back in 1991. When we got there, Liam Howlett was playing different
versions of the live show they were scheduled to headline the next day at
Ultra Music Festival. Prodigy's manager was arguing about which version
of "Smack My Bitch Up" they would play. I couldn't believe my ears. It was
the most insane remixes of Prodigy's own music, and Sandra and I kept
staring at each other as if this were a dream. At least for me, it was. I never
in my life thought I'd end up "partying" with Prodigy.

After that amazing experience, I got to speak at the technology panel,
and that year, my subject was Surround Sound music in DVD and HD
audio. After the presentation, I was approached by the marketing director for IOSONO sound, a German audio software and hardware manu-

facturer. This would be the culmination of my journey in "frequency." Another rather lengthy NDA was presented to me by IOSONO Sound's CEO, Uwe Karbenk. After signing, I was told about the future of surround or multichannel sound mixing, which was "no channel" mixing at all. IOSONO sound was developed by German electrical engineer and mathematician Dr. Karlheinz Brandenburg, the developer of mp3 audio data compression. He is also known for his elementary work in the field of audio coding, perception measurement, and wave-field synthesis and psychoacoustics, which has netted him numerous national and international research awards, prizes and honors.

I was hired to compose dance music for their sound system, which was at an undisclosed location of Disney Imagineering division. The system consisted of a "belt" of 340 self-powered speakers all around the cinema theater. The concept was simple: Through complex algorithms, the software recreates "natural sound" as it travels through space, while psychoacoustics and perception measurements "fool our brains," allowing the system to reproduce sound as it happens in real life. Put another way, IOSONO Sound is capable of having sound come from everywhere in the room, just as in everyday existence. Uwe said I should compose a piece exclusively for the IOSONO system, which was a crazy idea with limitless possibilities. I produced a track called "Paradise," which became a staple demo piece for them in their global marketing. Impressed with my work composing, IOSONO's CEO hired me to consult for potential alliances with destination venues.

The next year at WMC, I was given some news by my friend, Cliff Ward, who was the sales manager at Imagic, the creators of the Logic Pro music-production software. He was beaming, saying Apple Computers had recently bought them. I was asked to have dinner with Xander Soren, who is the man responsible for a then-tiny concept now known as iTunes. He said that I could do presentations for Apple promoting the first Apple Logic Studio. The problem was, I could do about 100 times more with a Dell PC laptop equipped with an Intel processor than any Mac with an IBM Powerbook could ever do.

Nevertheless, I embarked on a new quest with sound frequencies and Apple, heading to Las Vegas Consumer Electronic Show, COMDEX and E3 in L.A. During the time in Las Vegas, I met Gino Lopinto, owner of The Empire Ballroom (formerly the "Utopia" dance club), next to the MGM hotel. Gino, being a musician himself and a huge electronic music fan, along with a group of investors from San Diego, started a trend by bringing major DJs to Vegas for the first time, and the dance-club community from Miami as a casino revenue source, apart from gambling. Gino was the CEO of the Vegas Alliance, and because of my connections in the technology field, he hired me to showcase Apple Logic Pro and IOSONO sound and I became the VP of Technology for the first Vegas Music Conference.

This has been a personal journey as well as a professional one. The prophetic "frequencies" of Josh Wink's "Higher State Of Consciousness" that changed the way I experience sound many decades ago at Magic Wednesdays have gone on to change our world. "Frequencies" are in mainstream pop culture everywhere, be it in movies, TV, gaming, commercials, or the Internet. My belief is that the sensation of "frequencies"—highs and lows combined with rhythms—challenge our senses in new ways, creating spiritual awakenings through sound waves.

Today, my life has gone full circle. When I was a kid, there were no schools for electronic music or anything my brain could find to build a path to a music career with no musical abilities of my own. However, now I find myself going to school to learn about the next level of "frequencies": I'm studying towards a degree in metaphysics.

14 LENA ATOMIKA ('95)

Lena Atomika has been a raver, go-go dancer, photographer, actress, and a graduate of Second City.

I started out in Cleveland, Ohio, as a go-go dancer at a few dance clubs, including Metropolis and Aquilon...literally two of the best clubs in the Unites States at the time. The events thrown at these venues, among others, would attract the likes of Keoki and the "Club Kids" (like the now-notorious Michael Alig and his crew from New York City), Moby, Lady Miss Kier from Deee-Lite, and so on. I even remember the first issue of URB Magazine, which documented these clubs and parties...I probably still have that issue sitting around somewhere. Those involved with URB have gone on to become huge personalities in the rave and dance music culture, such as Jason Bentley and his long-running radio show "Metropolis" (props!) on Los Angeles KCRW 88.9FM, where he is now the Program Director.

I ended up moving to Los Angeles myself in 1995, and almost immediately discovered the underground dance culture after becoming a go-go dancer at The West End in Santa Monica. The owner was a British guy named Johnny, and the bouncers were the biggest and best-looking bouncers around (not to mention great guys), also British, except for one who happened to be from Cleveland, too. They had the best thumping beats, fresh from the U.K...many off the amazing "Hooj Choons" label. I remember the early days of Christopher Lawrence and Sandra Collins, who spun there from time to time as well. It was always a fun vibe and a great atmosphere...solid light show and lots of people grooving on the dance floor. Man, they played some wonderful house and techno there...I really miss those days!

And of course, those underground rave parties were AMAZING!!! The parties just got bigger and bigger, and attracted more and more people...they were quite the spectacle, in an amazingly beautiful and special way!

There were all kinds of parties, put on by all kinds of people...Insomniac, Wicked, Go Ventures, F.A.M.I.L.Y., Zodiac, just to name a few. Locations ranging from underground warehouse spaces, big and elaborate dance clubs and the Los Angeles Coliseum even, to outdoor locations in the desert and the mountains. And I had the opportunity to dance at most of them, both as a go-go dancer and as an attendee. It was always a new and exciting location and experience, with tons of people coming from all over. People would drive for hours to get to a party, and still do. One of the things I could usually count on, besides dancing for hours (because I LOVE it sooo much!), was always running into people I knew...it was like a big family...a community. People took care of each other and looked out for one another.

And there was lots of eye and ear candy, including fantastic laser shows (many done by Eye Candy Lasers), and several dance genres to choose from…drum and bass, techno, house, jungle, psytrance, etc. One of the best parties I ever went to was in Oakland, CA. It was a "Wicked" party…

The author on a Santa Monica dance floor.
Photo: Michael Tullberg

and oh yes, it lived up to its name! We danced ALL night, and I remember having to wring out my (excuse me) underwear, because they were soaking wet from all the sweat. It didn't help that I wore a vinyl dress that night!

Another memorable party was the "Right to Dance" protest event, held at the Federal Building in Westwood, L.A. I remember getting up on the speakers to dance and feeling the deep bass of the music, which was undoubtedly sending vibrations through the concrete of that whole structure. It was a huge turnout...a powerful testament by our community, expressing our deep love of music and dance.One of the coolest resources at the time (besides the tried-and-true rave flyer), were the underground dance hotlines that you could call to get a list of pretty much ALL the events happening in the area...it was so awesome! And then once you got the event location, it usually entailed going to a map point where you could purchase your ticket...ha ha, "old school style"!

One of the best things from those days was (and still is) the long-term friendships that were forged. To this day, I am still friends with many of those with whom I danced the night/morning/day away...such special times, for which I am so ever grateful! Friends like Helen O. & Dora, Sandie W., Todd T., Dimitri D., Neil T., & Bryan F. (RIP), and DJs such as Jason Blakemore, Taylor, Grant Plant, & Holly Adams, to name just a few. And, of course, the OG photographer himself, Michael Tullberg (the creator of this book). Those times and memories are very special and our connections run deep...I have a lot of LOVE for those folks! ☺ xoxo

15 JASON JAY - MAGIC WEDNESDAYS ('95)

Jason Jay is a Los Angeles-based promoter and musician, who was one of the founders of the Hollywood rave nightclub "Magic Wednesdays".

The truth of the matter is that behind every great music scene in American history is not a party, not a concert...but a club. Every one.

American psychedelic rock found its home in The Whisky in Hollywood with the Doors and the Byrds. Punk rock in America would never have become a culture without CBGB's in New York City hosting The Ramones and Blondie. Disco would never have become a national phenomenon without NYC's Studio 54. Heavy metal would never have hit the top of the charts without Motley Crue and Van Halen having a home at Gazzarri's on Sunset Boulevard. The list goes on and on.

That's what Magic Wednesdays gave to American electronic dance music. Not just a house, but a home—in a club.

In the late '80s to early '90s, there was the first wave of the rave scene that was boiling up from the underground. The original founders of the rave scene (people like Tef Foo, Gary Richards, Kool-Aid, Philip Blaine, Daven Michaels, Baba Lou, Gary Blitz and the Levy Brothers, to name a few) broke into warehouses in the downtown L.A. area and would throw sizable parties. That went on for a few years, along with a lot of problems, with parties being broken up all the time by law enforcement, and by 1992, the scene had almost completely died.

But out of the ashes came even larger parties, with thousands of people seeking the allure of the underground experience, now seductively taboo like the speakeasies of the Jazz Age. Parties now had an element of rebellion against the system that sought to end them.

Within a few short months in late 1992, the momentum was shut down again by authorities, after a promoter (who will not be named) broke into a warehouse owned by a city council member and trashed the place. We literally went from partying straight from Wednesday night until Monday morning to not knowing where to go. A scene of a couple of hundred people had blossomed to over five thousand in 1992, and then collapsed to even fewer than before due to a variety of issues, ranging from promoter irresponsibility to intense police and political pressure to crush rave music. These were definitely dark days indeed.

But a few of us…we happy few…still loved the music with everything we had, and a seed formed that would grow into a huge loving family.

One of the few places people could go to listen to this amazing electronic music was a Monday nighter called "The Ambient Lounge" with DJ Eli Star at the helm, at a Hollywood restaurant called Louis XIV located right off Melrose Avenue. The location was beautiful, the environment was world-class, the food was awesome and the music was epic…but in the beginning, very few people showed up until AuroMichael and I took over promotion. Within a few months, there were lines around the block to get in, and it felt like something special was happening as the scene was starting a new phase. The owners of the old Carlos'N Charlie's on the Sunset Strip took notice and asked us to relocate the weekly party to their venue. This is what gave birth to Magic Wednesdays.

Jason Jay (Top left) at an early edition of Magic Wednesdays.
Photo: Michael Tullberg

Within a month, the new place was packed, with hundreds of people lining up every week to listen to some of the most innovative electronic dance music on the planet. To understand the context of this, nothing else of this caliber on a weeknight was going on in Los Angeles clubs. Magic Wednesdays popped with an energy that was different from that found in any other venue. From the amazing flyers produced by core member Kay Moonstar, to the unlimited energy of the promoters, to the world-class spinning of Eli Star, this was a place unlike any other at a time when virtu-ally nothing else like it was happening in the city.

The scene coalesced around Magic Wednesdays, not only because of its amazing vibe and production, but because of its stability. It gave all of us wounded warriors of the dance scene a home, and maybe more importantly, a place to promote. A place to build. We offered a space for American and international artists to showcase themselves in what would become the West Coast's premier dance community. It was a major pillar upon which the body of the West Coast rave scene was built.

Pasquale Rotella, the mastermind behind Insomniac Productions, could be seen every Wednesday outside the front doors, personally handing out his flyers for what would one day become a worldwide brand. Inside, the experience was uniquely special, and we core producers were caught up riding the wave we were creating. Each night, AuroMichael and I would move throughout the space, cleansing the atmosphere with the burning of herbs and sending out good energies to the people so they would have a life-changing positive experience every time…AND THEY DID!

But here's the thing: At the time, we didn't realize that we were creating history. We were doing this out of pure love and we were just riding the wave that we helped create.

Magic Wednesdays became the West Coast hub for bringing talent from all over the world to celebrate this new form of music - electronic music. We had acts such as Bjork, Goldie, Sven Vath, Laurent Garnier, Rabbit in the Moon, Uberzone, Doc Martin, Electric Sky Church, The Crystal Method, Loop Guru, Death in Vegas, David J of Love and Rockets, Superstar DJ Keoki, DJ Dan, Donald Glaude, AK1200 and Juno Reactor, just to name a few. They showcased their fantastic skills (sometimes unannounced) in rooms exploding with energy, creating lifetime memories for those lucky enough to witness the sounds and energies of these amazing artists.

There was a miracle being created every Wednesday night. It came out of nowhere and it changed the L.A. music world. Such amazing, explosive, exciting, innovative times. An era when everything was new and people were driven by what they loved, and you could absolutely feel that love and innovation everywhere. And people flocked to our Wednesday nights from all over the world - it had become a destination.

Throughout Hollywood's creative industry, people made the journey to Magic Wednesdays. For many of them it was a first taste of these sounds that weren't rock 'n' roll or rap or pop: it was something new. People from all kinds of entertainment companies came to Magic Wednesdays, and you could soon see the impact in advertising, commercials, design, film and television, and of course, modern music. They were inspired by what they found in the club and began using elements of it in their professional output. It was similar to how Studio 54 helped the New York-based media saturate the public with disco in the late '70s.

As if all this wasn't enough, there was something special bubbling up in London in the early '90s that America had no idea about, called jungle and drum and bass. It was a new sound that AuroMichael had brought to the forefront in L.A.'s electronic music movement.

Magic Wednesdays established the first jungle room in a major American club. People had never heard this kinetic sound before; as far as they knew, it may have well come from Mars...and they LOVED IT. Soon URB Magazine was pushing drum and bass, you'd hear it on KCRW (usually during Jason Bentley's "Metropolis" show), and then it was finding its way into soundtracks of major films and games and such.

Eventually, we had to move to accommodate the enthusiasm and ever-growing crowds, and after bouncing here and there, ended up at a prime location in the heart of Hollywood. It was The World/The Ruby at 7070 Hollywood Boulevard, where the magic would go on for many years!

Through the '90s, 7070 Hollywood Blvd would hold over 1,500 people and was sold out almost every time. Magic Wednesdays was not only packed inside—people were lined up around the block just to hang outside, because they knew their friends would be along at some point that evening. It was the Mecca of Dance. It's where the world came to dance, AND THEY DID!

As it turned out, Magic Wednesdays' success was just one of the indicators of the massive expansion of the rave scene at the end of the decade. The scene was changing as people began gravitating to central events like our club, while parties like Audiotistic and Nocturnal Wonderland shed their underground status and became "events" and then later "concerts," before finally evolving into "world-changing festivals" in the new millennium.

The truth is that international festivals like ACA World Sound and Ultra, which now attract hundreds of thousands of people, would never have had a chance to become such massive phenomena if it were not for places like Magic Wednesdays. Its stability and quality provided an incubator for the grassroots that turned into a true cultural movement, which then spread across the land and changed everything.

The promoters of Magic Wednesdays put a lot of love and care into making sure everybody had not just an amazing time, but had the time of their lives. We wanted to create memories that would last forever and ever in everyone's mind, body and spirit, as well as remembering one thing: "We are all one."

It wasn't just a good time. For most who attended, it was also a spiritual experience that changed their lives forever and with it, the world, we think for the better.

Live in love.

Written with Jon Michael Kavulic and Dennis Irwin.

16 ERIN BROOKS - BASSICS ('96)

Erin Brooks is a veteran of desert raving in the American southwest.

When you think of Arizona raves, or desert raves, it's likely your mind draws up a dark and dusty, barren landscape – desolate, except for the spiraling glow sticks and glint of whistles, and those giant plastic pacifiers competing with kandi necklaces and white Vicks masks for that 2 inches of neck space. Vicks masks: In old rave footage, you might catch a glimpse of people wearing those white masks they give out at the doctor's office when you have a cough; smeared on the inside was Vicks VapoRub. There was something about the Vicks aroma that made the effects of Ecstasy super-amazing. In real life, it seemed like everyone had a mask on, even though the videos only show a few.

Yes, those desert raves happened and they were a blast! However, this story is about the adventure of finding the rave; the allure of discovery. For me, this one particular night brought to life everything so fascinating about techno and the rave scene – transcendence, that feeling of searching on the edge of monumental progress, a breakthrough in consciousness, cosmic awareness, and mindshift.

We were invited to this new realm through the music, with the beats, the complexity and dialogue between sounds and rhythm, the DJ names, song titles, names of the parties, names of the promoters, the mesmerizing album art, and the rave flyers...all of which combined the natural beauty of science with technology by using hypnotic, computer-generated art. Remember, it was all so new at the time. This marriage of science and technology quite literally paralleled my life through art and soundwaves, as I was a music-lover studying science and my husband had just started his computer-programming career.

We found new underground music by listening to our local alternative station late at night, by browsing independent shops like Swell, and by sound-swapping our new finds with friends. In the local directories, Swell was listed as just a record store with some clothing, but to the rest of us, it was our lifeline to the best music, futuristic styles, and the most vibrant parties. I chose raves based on the music, the DJs, flyer artwork, promoter, the name of the party, and the message; they were all pretty interconnected. Here's part of the small-print message on the flyer for a party called Bassics: "...it's time to come together, put aside the politics, and get down to 'Bassics'...[this] is the true spirit of why we throw parties, it's not about the politics, the money, drugs or the clothes you wear...it's about the music!"

Bassics was one of my first raves, and if I could go back to any one rave, it would be this one, a million times over! I was 21 and had just moved back to the Phoenix area with my husband and daughter to finish college, and had reconnected with my friend, KB, from high school, who I credit with taking me to my very first rave less than a year before.

Bassics was also my first outdoor rave, the largest rave I had ever been to, and to this day, the only rave where I've gathered with thousands of people under hundreds of towering Ponderosa pines. Headlining was Uberzone, a legend from California whose infinitely complex and intricate rhythms I had only heard from my home and car stereo speakers, and whose sound was immediately discernable from everyone else's in my music collection. Also headlining was Aux 88 from Detroit and Soul Oddity from Florida, both amazing, non-local, new discoveries for me.

(I actually had to look up the original rave flyer to make sure my memory was correct, so big thanks to the old-school rave group on Facebook and especially my friend, EV, who was similarly moved by rave culture and has since dedicated a massive amount of time and effort to collecting and preserving the lost art of rave flyers in an online archive.)

After shopping for the just-right attire, which included my favorite superfine iridescent body glitter, Hard Candy iridescent sparkly nail polish I bought at the Diesel store on Mill Avenue near my college, my miniskirt dress, white patent leather go-go boots, and kandi necklaces supplied by KB, we were dressed for a Central Phoenix warehouse party and ready to call the hotline to get directions! It was an easy-enough night to plan, since it was only she and I going; we didn't have to wait for a bunch of other friends to show up or pick anyone up on the way.

The rave flyers we picked up at Swell or previous parties would have a phone number listed where we could only call within twenty-four hours of the party to find out the location. We'd gather around and listen with anticipation to the excited, fuzzy recordings— we would have it on "speaker" or one of us would have our ear to the receiver while the other jotted down directions. Then we'd set out to find our way. The search was like a scavenger hunt, our path confirmed when we'd catch glimpses of other ravers, and our imminent arrival confirmed when we'd hear the music and feel the thunderous bass lines.

This particular party mentioned some exit we estimated to be way out in North Phoenix, which was only about thirty minutes away from my Tempe apartment.

We drove from the I-10 west and north along the orange-lit I-17, looking out at the urban expanse, dotted with thousands of twinkling speckles of porch lights, streetlights, and shimmering headlights, all dotted and sprawled in rows along the valley floor and streaming upward onto the surrounding foothills and mountains.

We kept driving until we broke free from that dome of city light, into the darkness of the desert, where the stars become innumerable, and the sparse, low-lying shrubs multiply, gradually filling in the gaps of the pale, fine-clay, desert concrete.

We knew we were far from home when we'd see the soil turn a darker brown, until there was no more caliche and the wispy desert shrubs would fill in, standing a foot taller at each mile marker until they eventually became towering evergreen trees. About an hour north, we stopped at a mom & pop gas station in the middle of nowhere to use the payphone to call the hotline again and double-check our directions. While doing this, we spotted a low-rider truckload of ravers who hopped out blowing whistles and wearing Vicks masks, so we talked with them briefly to make sure we weren't lost, and then kept going, knowing we were close.

The temperature dropped as we kept going further north and higher up out of the desert valley. The night sky was clear, but became even darker as we ventured toward Flagstaff at exit 300-something. Our anticipated thirty-minute trip had now taken about two hours of driving at this point.

We finally saw the small sign directing us from alongside the highway and lively people our age dressed warmly in beanies and gloves, waving us into park in rows between the trees; a new adventure in itself for this city girl! Growing up surrounded only by urban and suburban infrastructure, with nearly no nature, and with public transportation at nearly every corner, made this particular rave trek all the more adventuresome and transformative for me as we drove while constantly reflecting on our own love of the music.

So for my first adventure, I expected a typical concert experience, where lots of fans gather and enjoy the music. Yeah, there was definitely music with lots of people gathered, but in rave crowds, there were infinitely more whistles and glow sticks, and we weren't so focused on watching the performer as much as enjoying our personal experience with the performance that was gifted to us by the DJ artists.

Everyone interacted with the music differently: Some would gather around to watch someone's new moves, while some people liked building an audience so that they could show off their own moves. Some would cozy up to the speakers and some would line up around the perimeters of the various areas, or off to the sides where they would talk and socialize more than anything. As with any social gathering, there was a lot going on, and we connected through the music; it brought us together. What kept us coming back was that connection with each other, to be in a space with so much friendliness and pure joy! The community, the camaraderie, compassion, PLUR – peace, love, unity, respect; people from all different groups getting along and being nice to each other, not just not fighting, but actually being *kind* to one another. Those interactions sort of blew my mind. It's true there were drugs; I can't pretend there weren't. I imagine it was similar to the hippie days, where at raves, the drugs of choice soothed angst and aggression to the point of compassion and respect. It was absolutely lovely.

My favorite part of Bassics was standing at the back of the crowd as we first arrived, welcomed by the colored lasers that were scanning the pine forest as excitedly as a pair of glow sticks snarled in between the fingers of the ravers, and massive bass with an interstitial resonance delivered to each of us, tugging us into the crowd by our waists. It must have been about midnight, and we got there just in time to hear Uberzone's basswave level the tall pines—a memory I hope to never forget! In my mind, I see the deep sound wash over us like a wave. The experience of hearing him in person was as life-affirming as I had dreamed…look up his stuff, or Botz from the Hardhop Trypno compilation from Moonshine. Standing there, wrapped in that finely woven swath of the sizzle and crisp pop of the snare, which comprised his signature, multi-layered, musical textures. Then the BOOM, the explosive bass. It was just too good to be real!

We all just moved along with the music and enjoyed the vibe, no snide looks or comments or cliques, just everyone happy and having a blast! Everyone was so very friendly! Back in the '90s, people (where I grew up in AZ, anyway) were divided by every imaginable category, line, measure, whatever…there were divisions. I wasn't used to people of different groups coming together under the same roof, or sky even, and actually getting along with each other, like smiling and interacting in respectful, humane ways. It was beautiful and gave us optimism for the future, seeing that people really could get along and our perceived and constructed divisions were pointless.

Of course, at Bassics, I was freezing my bleepity-bleep off, as we'd brought no hats, gloves or jackets, and were clearly unprepared for the Northern Arizona chill. Our car ended up getting stuck in a ditch until a super-nice bus driver helped us tow it out. Actually, my friend reminded me that he was kind of grouchy about helping us at first, but our only other option was to call AAA, which we couldn't do, because we couldn't let anyone know we were out there! It was an illegal party, after all, and we didn't want to be the ones responsible for making the cops show up!

The night turned out to be a swirl of energy, positivity, glow sticks, smiles, whistles, jumping, colorful colors, bass, all the techno genres with their complex beats. Especially exhilarating was how all the people were from different groups, ages, sizes, shapes, colors! Every colorful color. Everyone was SO colorful! Everyone dressed in bright gleaming smiles and brilliant primary colors, and our jeans fit loosely around the legs for lots of movement. My favorite rave attire was my bright yellow, long-sleeved skinny Polo mock T-neck under my Dickies overalls, sized humongous, and cut off at the hem. How much I wished I had worn those instead that night!

All of the music that night was fantastic, and the local support at parties was well-received; the local DJs were Gary Menichiello, Emile, and Bahumut. There was something for everyone, with a mix of house, trance, breakbeat, jungle, hardcore. Those were just a few of the '90s genres; new evolutions of music come and go, but it seems they branch off from some of these original points. Our local alternative station kept us connected and up all night into the early mornings with great mixes from DJs around town and from all over the world.

On our way back to Phoenix, in those early-morning hours, we drove listening to one of the local DJ sets playing on the alternative station to stay awake, then stopped off at a rest stop and snuggled ourselves up in our seats with blankets and took a shallow nap as the sun rose.

Keep in mind, this adventure happened back when cell phones weren't really a thing yet. I only had a landline in my apartment and it was useless, because the computer gamers in my life kept it buzzing 24/7, since this was also at a time before hi-speed internet connections. So I called home several times, but the line was busy. Gamers.

At about 7:00 AM, the sun peeked up over the pine tops and mountain peaks, and the brilliant morning yellows, oranges, and reds were as vibrant and piercing to our eyes in our haze of sleep deprivation as the lasers were just a few short hours prior.

When I got back to my classes early Monday, I tried to carry on as if my life had not just been altered forever. I had no idea how profoundly that night, and the rave scene for the next few years to come, would greatly impact my interactions with others and my life choices. Think about it: Peace. Love. Unity. Respect. We're never too old to rave.

Thank you for reading, and much love to you <3

17 MARGARET SCHLAMP - FREAKNIGHT ('08)

Margaret Schlamp is a resident of the Pacific Northwest and a huge fan of trance music.

Two of my favorite quotes, from people who have influenced our culture for all time, in my opinion, are what rave festivals are all about:

"We dance for laughter, we dance for tears, we dance for madness, we dance for fears, we dance for hopes, we dance for screams, we are the dancers, we create the dreams." –Albert Einstein

"Music doesn't lie. If there is something to be changed in this world, then it can only happen through music." –Jimi Hendrix

This is my rave journey, my raver story that has transformed my life forever.

I am 56 years old, and from 1974 to the present day, dance music has always been part of my life. I've been listening and dancing to this incredible, massive music, including techno, trance, house and other genres for 40+ years, and I'm looking forward to many more.

My dance journey of embracing rave…Peace, Love, Unity, Respect

(PLUR) began in 1970. At ten years old, my Abuelita ("Grandmother" in Spanish) gifted me a transistor radio. Thumbing thru radio stations, I came across one named KJR that aired disco, progressive rock, funk and soul music. I loved the lyrics and the variety of bangin' beats that would go right thru your soul. I also watched the weekly TV programs "American Bandstand" and "Soul Train," shows that featured musical artists, singers and dancers that boogied to the music I listened to on the radio. It was so groovy.

In '74, when I was fourteen, some radio stations began airing early dance/club music. WoW! I'd never heard of this type of music before, and it was so addicting that I couldn't get enough! In those days we Baby Boomers went to the record store to purchase music, as we didn't have the luxury of the Internet, social media, Spotify, etc., to download and enjoy the music like we do today. And of course, trance/dance/EDM festivals were not in existence yet in my neck of the woods. I would go with my hard-earned money to a local record store in Seattle named Bob Street Records, and another in my neighborhood in West Seattle named Easy Street Records to buy my 45s, 8-tracks, cassette tapes and LPs. This would eventually come to include music by DJs like Dieselboy, Frankie Knuckles, Eddie Amador, Giorgio Moroder, Omar Santana, Moby, C & C Music factory, and many more. It's massive get-down music!

To this day, I periodically pay record stores a visit and purchase dance/ club music. When I walk through the doors, I can practically smell the music history, and I'm always excited with anticipation as to what treasures I will find.

In the '80s and '90s, I would dance the night away at nightclubs or discotheques—yes, with the huge rotating disco ball hanging from the ceiling and lasers bouncing all over the mirrored walls! This was called "clubbing" instead of "raving." As the years went by, and with the explosion of the Internet, I read about these huge dance events occurring in Europe and the UK called "raves." I thought, "What in the heck is a rave? What was I missing out on?" So I did my research online and I concluded that the word "clubbing" from the '80s correlated to the "rave" of the '90s. That is, a massive amount of people enjoying trance, underground, and different genres of electronic music played by DJs at big dance festivals, lasting from one day/night to all day/night/day. This struck me as something wonderful, and I thought, "How cool is that! WoW! Boy, I want to be part of this rave movement!"

On one of my visits to one of the record stores in the late '90s (I can't remember which one—yes, brain burp), I came across an LP named "45 RPM" by Paul van Dyk. Scratching my head, I was curious as to what it sounded like, so I asked the clerk if he could play it. OMG! I nearly fell out of my shoes, because I was in trance heaven! I grabbed it, bought it and it's mine, and is still in my media library collection. I looked around the store and asked if he had more LPs from Europe. He pointed to a section located in the back corner of the store. By golly, this section was HUGE! Oh man, I could spend a day and a year browsing and reading the sleeves of these LPs. I mean, artists like G.T.O, Ferry Corsten, DJ (Groovemaster) Johnson, La Bouche, Scumfrog, EON, The Prodigy, Cosmic Baby, Gordon Kaye and LFO. When I would play them, I'd close my eyes and feel the beat of the music go thru my soul, transporting me to euphoric trance heaven, and it still does to this day. Trance music is my drug indeed.

I went to my very first massive U.S. dance festival in 2008: the annual circus-themed EDM Halloween rave named FreakNight Festival, sponsored by the United State Of Consciousness (USC). It's held every Halloween weekend here in Seattle and it's been the largest EDM/dance festival here in the Pacific Northwest for years. I thought to myself, "Dang,

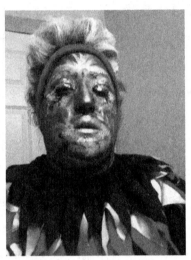

The author, ready to go. Self-portrait.

I want to go really bad to FreakNight and dance the night away with my fellow trance family." My overriding wish was to see these awesome DJ artists perform! My problem was, I didn't have anyone to go with, as my family and friends aren't into trance music. I've invited them to go to see what it's all about. My family would tell me that I'd lost my mind, and they still do.

There have been two separate unforeseen tragedies that occurred in my family. They were the passing of two of my younger siblings in 1995 and 2007. To give myself a mental break from the grief after my second bereavement, I got the courage to attend the FreakNight Festival in '08 in their honor and memory. At 48 years old, my wish finally became a reality.

It was a very, very cold, brisk and clear Halloween night. As I pulled my car into the parking lot at the Washington Mutual (WAMU) Theatre, I was very apprehensive, because I'd never seen so many people. Even at a distance, I could hear the deep beat of the music radiating through the pavement and in the air. It was so loud, I felt intimidated and wanted to turn around, get into my car and drive away. What was I getting myself into? I thought for a second and said to myself, "Wait! I've got nothing to lose, so let's go have some fun." I was looking forward to seeing the legend of trance, Paul van Dyk, Moby and many more. So with my VIP ticket, ID, camera and purse in hand, confident me walked towards the theater.

As I walked past the huge main line and headed towards the VIP entrance, lots of people gave me high fives, because they liked my scary Halloween jester costume and makeup. That was so cool! I now felt at ease, and could feel the party vibes, and the music pulsing in the air and through my body. As I approached the entrance, which was decorated with brilliant circus-themed colored lights, I felt as if I was a young girl going to a fall state fair at night, but without my parents! Pure excitement and anticipation! WoW! It was truly intoxicating! Security cleared me, I walked in, and was just simply amazed at the spectacle of it all.

At first, I was at ground level and could barely see the DJs performing, but watching jugglers performing to ringmasters walking on eight-foot stilts, and dancers and acrobats hanging high from the ceiling and dancing to the music was incredible! There were tons of people wearing Halloween costumes of all types. I saw scary skeletons, zombies like from the show "The Walking Dead," ballerinas, a person dressed like the Pope, nuns, scary clowns, and so many creative costumes that had no category to place them in. Some hilarious, and some that would make you scratch your head and say "What the hell?" or "You've got be kidding me!" or "OMG!" I even saw someone dressed like "Jack" from Jack In The Box, who kept walking into things, because he couldn't see! I was laughing my head off! Let your imagination run wild, and most likely you will see it in the flesh at FreakNight Festival.

I spotted the VIP section, walked up the stairs, and was given a special VIP lanyard to wear at all times. I felt so important! I saw spectacular colorful laser lights dancing all over the place. I leaned over the railing and could literally see a massive sea of people dancing in unison. How exciting this was! Simply jaw-dropping! The venue shook to the beat of the music and people dancing! I'd never experienced anything like this! This was so mind-blowing! I was in sheer bliss! What a way to be introduced to this beautiful new world!

This amazing experience convinced me to attend more FreakNights— some were awesome, others less so. At the 2012 edition, there were two ladies dancing with me, and they asked if I would like some rave bracelets or kandis. I said sure, not knowing what they signified. They took my hands, and as our fingers entwined, they explained the meaning of the kandis as we made symbols with our hands signifying Peace, Love, Unity, Respect (PLUR), promoting the values of rave festivals. I thanked them and danced the night away with my new friends, my fellow trance family. The king of trance, Armin Van Buuren, was spinning an incredible set that even had the VIP security dancing. That is, until the power went out and killed his performance, which was crushing…fortunately, Armin would return in the future.

A couple of years later, a young kid sadly died during the first night of the two-day event. I felt really bad for the family who lost their loved one, and worse when Century Link (who runs WAMU) cancelled the second night without informing any of the attendees. They could have handled that better, for sure. From then on, FreakNights moved to the Tacoma Dome, outside of Seattle.

At the most recent FreakNight in 2016, USC celebrated their 20-year anniversary. I dedicated this special two-day rave event to my precious Mom, who had recently passed from cancer. She loved to dance and I knew she was with me in spirit. There were so many local and international DJ artists performing at this festival and it was incredible! My mind was spinning…talk about massive, and I mean MASSIVE!!! Feeling the festival vibes and the excitement of it all, and experiencing these magical nights with my fellow trance family are the best feelings in the world.

I befriended one of the coolest local DJ duos from here in Seattle, Sean and Xander. I was absolutely excited when I read on FreakNight's Facebook page that they were included in the lineup, so I direct-messaged them for a meet-and-greet. "Absolutely," they said. I was so freaking excited! We met up at one of the stages and had a great chat, took some pictures, and they autographed my banner, too! They made my night so special!

At the Main Stage area, the place was packed to the rafters. From the VIP section, I could see mounds and mounds of people trying to wiggle their way around in this HUGE venue to get a good view to see Armin van Buuren perform. At VIP, we weren't close to the stage, but the section was high enough in that you could see the stage just above the crowd. You really needed binoculars to clearly see what was happening, and thank God I brought mine!

At the beginning before he appeared on the stage, you heard the cackle of a scary witch: "Ahe, hae, hae, hae, hae, hae!" as the music started. Armin wore a black T-shirt with a scary, orange Halloween pumpkin design on it. His face had a zipper that opened from between his eyebrows to his cheeks, and greenish ghoulish guck covered the top of his nose to his chin. His Halloween costume gave me the willies—he looked really creepy! There were lots of Halloween-themed LED lights in the backdrop and around the front of the stage, which made it appear like Armin was performing in a picture frame of light. This was pretty cool, especially when they would incorporate Armin's name within their designs. I'd never seen anything like it!

Then the music started to build and all hell broke loose. Everyone was dancing with Armin and the venue was shaking in unison to the beat, with everyone jumping up and down. Even the VIP platform was shaking! Armin put the venue in A State Of Trance—what a massive feeling! It was so fun dancing with my fellow trance family! I even saw Armin dancing his signature spin. Dang, this was incredible to see! At the end of his epic performance, the backdrop design showed Armin thanking Seattle along with "Embrace," referring to his album of the same name. What an awesome experience!

On top of that, I also saw the legend of trance, Paul van Dyk, perform at his stage. I was in sheer heaven, since as I said earlier, I've been listening and dancing to his music after discovering his "45 RPM" LP at that record store. He played a lot of his classics, and some current tracks, too. From the spectacular light designs in the backdrop to the magnificent colors of the lasers flying all over the place, I was in Vandit heaven! What a magical moment!

Just before he spun his last song, I made way to stage right. There were about five other people already waiting there, hoping for a meet-and-greet with Paul. His staff came up and told us, "Yes, but it's going to be brief." Talk about out-of-this-world excitement—to finally meet the legend! I couldn't believe it and I thought to myself, "What do I say? Just don't say anything stupid!"

We waited for around ten minutes, and then Paul appeared. We fans were looking at each other just giddy with excitement! He approached the metal barrier near the exit and started autographing items and taking pictures with us fans. I was the last person of the six to meet Paul. I was really nervous (and I mean *really* nervous) and star-struck. I couldn't believe I was finally meeting him! He came to me and I spoke to him, thanking him for sharing his love of music, and confessed that I'd been listening to his music since "45 RPM." I had my picture taken with Paul. He was so gracious and smiled a lot, and he autographed my banner! I thanked him for the meet and he smiled back! Then his staff escorted him to the exit. All six of us were jumping up and down—it was such a surreal moment! A special moment! I hope that in the future, I can meet Paul without wearing my Halloween costume, and to show him the many LPs he's released that are part of my media library. I will never forget this incredible moment for the rest of my life!

Periodically, I'm asked my age at parties. I'm flattered and blessed, because there is no age limit in dancing in intimate rave settings or huge locations. One year, a young gentleman was dancing beside me and he told me that he had been watching me jumping and dancing all night. With respect, he asked my age, and I responded proudly, "53 years old." He replied, "That's *awesome!*" and said that he hoped he could be dancing at my age. Then he gave me a hug and a high five! Throughout the years, when people ask my age and I tell them, they do that a lot. I'm always in disbelief in a good way and I smile from ear to ear.

At 56 years, I've been attending a lot of raves, and to those that say I'm crazy and too old to attend raves, I tell them to come with me and dance together with my fellow trance family; to enjoy these magical events and experience the festival vibes, the beat and melody of the music that these artists create. The feelings of joyfulness and the elation of it all, in the most colorful atmosphere possible, are the best feelings in the world! To escape from reality, with no judgment and no worries. To just be! Embracing rave…Peace, Love, Unity, Respect.

I really like this "rave" thing.

18 TALLY GROST ('96)

Tally Grost is a former hardcore raver who now occasionally spins as DJ Lunarsequence.

I first heard the term "rave" when I was in the fourth grade: I read a newspaper article in which underground, illegal dance parties were being held in warehouses that were broken into, and illicitly used for a night of fun and dancing and the absolute freedom of being your true self. I grew up dancing in dance classes and in my bedroom, and at the age of 38, I still haven't stopped dancing. It's an integral part of my being, and will be for the rest of my life. I first heard what was then called techno when I heard the song "James Brown is Dead" by L.A. Style. I loved it, and while my musical tastes have changed, it still brings back so many memories.

These two events basically made my eventual introduction to the electronic music scene destiny.

My first rave was in late summer/early fall of 1996 in El Paso, Texas, where I was born and raised. I still have the flyer; it was a Moontribe party at this rather divey (and now defunct) club named The Fog in a somewhat seedy part of town. I believe the headliner of this event was either

DJ Trevor or Petey. I didn't actually realize it was a Moontribe party until much, much later, as my knowledge of electronic music at that time was minimal at best. The club itself was very dark, and its namesake was appropriate as all I could see were shadows of people and fog. I had always envisioned raves as being filled with light and being welcoming but honestly, this event felt somewhat scary, but being that I was 17 and wanted to be cool and edgy, I went with it. I don't recall very much that night, but I knew I was hooked and wanted more.

I attended this party alone, but ended up meeting a girl who became a lifelong friend. Her name is Heather, and today she goes by Heather B when she spins deep house. She and I soon became almost inseparable, and while our musical interests have evolved into different genres, we still share a love of music and the rave scene. We attended a lot of different events together since that dark party in El Paso and have both moved around the country in similar patterns, serendipitously: first to Albuquerque, New Mexico, then to the Bay Area in California where Heather still resides and I plan to move back eventually.

Heather moved to Albuquerque a couple of years after we'd become friends, and I soon followed suit after having fallen for someone up there. Also, I was nineteen and needed to get away from my parents, and Albuquerque was close enough to home yet far enough away as well. I had met a large group of people from the New Mexico rave scene during the beginning days of the Internet, through a website called hyperreal.org. I and many other people I still call friends were members of the Mountain Raves section of that website, which focused on the scene in the Rocky Mountain region. I, too, hosted a website that I designed and programmed via HTML called Phunktified, where I collected all things rave and posted about upcoming and past parties. These two websites were the main catalysts for my move to New Mexico from West Texas.

I moved up there in the winter of 1998 shortly after my graduation from high school, and thereafter discovered the amazingness of central and northern New Mexican desert parties. I had moved up earlier than planned, because I had fallen for a man named Justin, who was a trance and progressive house DJ—we're still friends, by the way; he and another close DJ friend spun at my wedding. He and all of my other online rave friends introduced me to the scene and the people there, and I quickly and effortlessly became embedded and very much involved. I remember countless nights driving through the desert in the middle of nowhere, frequently stopping the car and turning off the engine so as to hear the bass from the speaker—this was in the days where map points were still a thing and you only had a general idea of where a desert party was to be held. You had to keep your eyes peeled looking for signs that were usually easy to miss.

Desert parties are something special. The idea of hundreds or thousands of people collectively dancing under the stars in the middle of nowhere gives me goosebumps to this day. The fact that these different people from all walks of life drove sometimes for hours for the same purpose to me is incredible. There is something so utterly transcendent about seeing the sunrise and noticing the natural beauty around you as you groove away to music that drives you to do nothing but dance and be in the moment. I have made lifelong friends because of this special counterculture.

I have spent countless nights dancing in the dirt amongst kindred spirits under the wide open western sky; I have been so deeply enthralled with the music that I was literally in a transcendental meditative state in which I felt a connection with the cosmos and all the life around—not just humans—without drugs. Yes, drugs were a part of the scene, just as they are a part of humanity, but these parties weren't about the drugs—they were about making connections with our world and each other through the common love of the beauty of the desert, dancing, raving, and underground dance music.

The author, self-portrait

For me, the best part of dancing all night and feeling at one with your planet and surroundings is the sunrise. The awakening of the sun brings about a sudden awareness of all that you missed while you danced in the dark; I have realized after hours that I was dancing in the middle of a plateau within mountains surrounded by a forest; I have realized I was dancing in the most gorgeous of high desert dunes that were indescribably beautiful and watercolors wouldn't come anywhere near painting it with justice.

My favorite of all the desert parties was Junebug, thrown every June by my good friend and DJ/Producer, Grant—a.k.a. Hotfoot or Esque. These parties always featured only local talent and kept the vibe small and intimate. I believe there were some parties that brought out larger numbers, but typically, only several hundred people attended these events. The vibe at Junebug was always amazing, up until the last one in 2006. That year, the party was thrown on an Indian reservation and all the proceeds were to benefit the community there. Unfortunately, raves were quickly becoming hotbeds of people seeking out drugs and drama, and a couple of gang members became involved in an altercation that ended with one person being stabbed and the party being shut down. Aside from that year, all the other events had been amazing and peaceful and nothing but positivity came from them.

For about ten years, I did nothing but work shitty jobs in order to fuel my rave lifestyle. I eventually started school at UNM, but I still managed to make it out over five nights a week. I ended up buying myself a pair of Technics 1200s with student-loan money and taught myself how to spin in 2002. I started playing at raves in Albuquerque and Santa Fe about a year later under the moniker Lunarsequence, which I still use to this day. I played dirty, dark progressive house and bass-driven breaks. I retired for a number of years but recently decided I missed playing and I have a new obsession with drum and bass, so I play that now, too.

I must say now that as I am older and my time is much more valuable, I rarely go out. I now get panic attacks amongst large crowds, so I much prefer smaller, more intimate events that have room to dance in. I'm also extremely particular about who I go see play. I personally find the words "soulful" and "deep" to be complete turnoffs; I'd rather hear some techy or dark drum and bass or progressive. I know exactly what I like and do not like and I am more about quality over quantity. Being a DJ has definitely changed my perception of music, as I have grown to become extremely picky. If the music sucks, I leave. I cannot dance if I do not feel it, and when I spin, I spin what I love. I refuse to play what I do not feel, and therefore I don't play out that much, which is fine by me.

I must say that the biggest night of my DJ career was playing an all-female show in El Paso where I opened for DJ Colette. I had an amazing night and played a great set that ended in me signing autographs and posing for pictures, which was surreal to say the least. That was the first time I had really rocked a crowd like that, and I felt a rush and a surge of adrenaline because of it. Unfortunately, after that I did not get booked again, which I am still unsure of as to why. I most recently played at a monthly event in El Paso called La Parada, which celebrates the border culture and features live art, local vendors, and a plethora of underground talent in all underground genres.

Living in the Bay Area solidified my obsession with drum and bass; the DnB scene there is world-famous, and I quickly discovered a free weekly event called Stamina Sundays in San Francisco. I attended that at least twice a month, usually alone, and met some amazing people there. It's held every Sunday come hell or high water in this tiny little club/art gallery called F8 near the Civic Center; some of the talent I've seen there includes AK1200, OM Unit, and Commix, among others. I quickly befriended the staff and made some lifelong friends there over the course of the two years I attended their shows. I think the reason I am now so much more drawn to drum and bass above all other genres is that it's remained relatively underground for the 25-ish years of its existence. People who love drum and bass REALLY love drum and bass, and the connected vibes at these shows mimic those of my earlier rave days.

The rave scene was a huge part of my life for years and helped shape me into the mover and shaker that I am today. I rarely go out now, but dancing is and will always be a necessary part of my life, because it is my addiction. Music drives everything that I do and I would be an empty shell without it. If I am in my car, I dance; when I listen to music at home, I dance; if I am lying down listening to music, I dance in my head. Dance and electronic music is me and always will be. It drives my creativity as a DJ, a visual artist, a cook and as a teacher, my current profession.

19 BRIAN JAMES - NEVER DOUBT THE HAT ('97)

Brian James is a Philadelphia resident and electronic music fanatic.

A well-respected Philly rave party crew called Circle were throwing a very massive event called "It." I had heard about these parties and I badly wanted to check one out. I'd found out about it from Nigel Richards, owner of 611 Records, on South Street. I asked where the flyer was and he said that they were all gone and there were only a few tickets left. I immediately bought two.

I called my best friend and told him that I had gotten us both tickets to a rave that was going to have Josh Wink, one of Philadelphia's many hometown DJ heroes. Now, I had heard Josh play at lots of raves, but I had heard that the "It" parties were just legendary. Every time one came up, I was unable to go, because I had to work or I heard about it after the fact. I wasn't going to miss seeing Josh at one of these amazing parties, so I managed to find out early enough about this event that I could request the weekend off. When we got there, the convention center was already full to the brim and they were only letting in people when other people inside were leaving. My friend was getting irritated.

"Man, I don't think we're getting in…" he said.

"Yes, we will." I replied. "Trust me. We're going to see Wink tonight, somehow!"

Another 20 minutes rolled by and the situation went from bad to worse. There were even more people now, and I saw one of the organizers of the party come out and explain that they were at capacity and they just

The author, self-portrait

couldn't fit any more people in. He apologized and explained that they'd set up a table to refund the tickets at full price.

"Well, I guess that's it," said my friend. "I knew it…Let's get in line."

Now, I happened to know that the hotel that's next door is attached to the convention center, and this was due to the many comic book conventions I went to there as a kid. As I got older, I found out that the hotel has a nightclub in the basement and I would stay after the club was closing, chatting with the DJs and helping them carry their records out once the club was finished cleaning up from that night.

"Nah, man. We're getting in." I explained sternly. "C'mon. Follow me."

My friend followed me, all the while asking about how this was going to work. I explained that I used to come to the club here and got to know the DJs well enough to be able to hang out afterwards and carry their records to their cars, by way of a back exit. It was this exit that we headed for.

"Ah! Here we are." I said.

"Yeah, and?!?" he blurts out. "I bet it's locked."

"Watch." I said in a determined voice, and I pulled the door open.

"Oh my God!" he quietly exclaimed. "Are you sure about this?!?"

"Trust the hat, bro." I replied, pointing to my purple, two-gloved, Anarchic Adjustment hat that I had bought on South Street in Philly as my moniker for when I went out raving or clubbing, and now as a way that people will recognize me when I DJ. I still wear it to this day, twenty-four years later.

We walked in the dark down the stairs to a door. I looked through the small square window and into the empty club on the other side. It was lit, but no one was in there, including the staff. I opened the door and we strolled on through.

"Whoa!" my friend said. "I had no idea there was a club in here!"

"Yeah, it was called 'Shadows' back in the day." I told him, "C'mon... over here." I motioned to a set of double doors on the other side of the club.

On the other side of these doors were banquet halls, and this time, there were staff in there putting tables away.

"Oh, we are SO screwed!" said my friend. "We ain't getting past these guys."

"Shhh!!" I said. "Just walk on through...they're just too busy to be worried about us." I quietly pushed the door open and we slipped through and walked right past the staff without question. I could hear my friend quietly giggling behind me, with the *"we're going to get caught"* frame of mind in his voice. We make it to the double doors on the other side and second banquet hall. It was empty and we strolled over to the next set of double doors.

I was grinning to myself as we walked through the curved hall where all the hotel's gift shops are, and past the stairs to the hotel lobby, where I could hear people upstairs checking in at the front desk. We arrived at yet another set of double doors and could start to make out the constant *thump-thump-thump-thump* of the kick drum from the main room now. We were on such a roll!

"No one is going to believe this story when we tell them!" I thought.

Through this set of double doors was the hotel's laundry area. We started to hear the techno music even more now. We began walking down the hall to the last set of doors, passing rooms on each side with giant industrial washing machines set up at the backs of them. All the while, I was quietly telling my friend, "Keep walking...do not stop."

Then we walked past one of the rooms and there was a heavyset security guard who was sitting down when he spotted us. We picked up the pace just a little as we heard him say, "HEY, YOU TWO!"

"Oh shit," says my friend. I could hear the guard drop his magazine and the foldable chair creaking loudly as he quickly got up to come face us.

"Let me do the talking," I said, as we turned around.

"Where do you two think you're going?!?" said the red-shirted guard, who seemed to have broken a sweat just getting up.

"Oh, we were looking for the bathroom, and got lost!" I happily blurted out. I could feel my friend looking at me as if to tell me that has to be the lamest excuse ever.

"No, no, no…there's no bathroom back here," says the guard waving his hand. "It's on the other side of the hall. Go through those doors and make a right, then a left. They're right by the soda machines." He pushed open the door, scooted us into the hallway next to the dance floor and finished with, "Have a good night now," as he went back to his post.

There were ravers everywhere and the music in the main area was now as clear as a bell! Other ravers who were camped out in the hall taking a break from dancing started to greet us, even though we didn't know them.

We'd done it! We'd gotten in, and we still had our full tickets! My friend and I laughed and laughed as we looked at each other in complete disbelief about what had just happened. We made our way over to the main room as we heard two bouncers talking about the mass of people still outside waiting and wanting to get in.

"Yo man, I ain't never seen this many kids!" said one bouncer to the other.

"Man! Do you realize that there's 400 MORE people outside?" the other one replied.

We strolled past them into the main hall and headed to the front towards the stage where the DJs were set up. We were there for no more than three minutes when we saw Josh Wink talking behind the current DJ. He noticed my friend and me and pointed at us, smiling and nodding positively. We didn't miss Wink's set! We were right on time! I was so relieved and so excited at the same time.

My friend leaned over, put his hand on my shoulder and said, "I will NEVER doubt the hat again!! We made it!!"

Wink went on and played a killer set. I remember him spinning "Disco Babes From Outer Space" by Babe Instinct, "Born Slippy" from Underworld, and of course Josh's own "Higher States Of Consciousness," the Tweekin Acid Funk Mix version with his expert hands-on 303 business at the back end of the song, which, when it dropped, the whole crowd had their hands up and everyone was dancing like their lives depended on it! Everyone smiled as we danced and raved on through the night and into the next morning. We came outside to a somewhat cloudy day and headed to my friend's house, where we crashed and went to sleep.

This really happened. I still have the ticket and I still wear the hat when I'm going dancing or if I'm DJing. This story still makes me smile, twenty-four years later. As always, thanks Josh!

20 MICHAEL TULLBERG - DUNE 4 ('98)

Michael Tullberg is a rave photojournalist and the editor of "The Raver Stories Project".

I've been driving for hours now, out into the middle of nowhere, to a distant location deep in the desert, somewhere near the California/Arizona border. This is by far the longest I've driven for just a one-night event, and part of me is asking myself just why the hell I'm doing this. Easy: three of my rave magazines are expecting pictures from this gig in the next couple of days! However, desert raving is something that in a lot of ways is completely different from any other kind of partying, and the Dune raves are supposed to be the best of the bunch, so I put my faith in that notion and push onwards into the darkness.

The gas needle is creeping precariously low. How long ago did I pass that last gas station? This is gonna be a nail-biter, getting out of here tomorrow morning...hope this is worth it.

Some time (and more than a few sweats) later, I finally get in, and thankfully I have a guest pass, so I can park in the tiny private area reserved for those working this gig. Getting there is something of an adventure unto itself, since I'm creeping along bumpy desert dirt roads that are filled with hidden holes and rocks. Still, it's a lot better than having to have to walk the 1-2 miles like most kids are being forced to do, that's for sure.

This is going to be a really good lineup tonight. Most of the desert-rave veteran DJs are here: Christopher Lawrence, Doran, Taylor, Thee-O, Bradley B, Brian, Robbie Hardkiss…yeah, this is going to be good. They have a thing for taking the atmosphere up to another level in places like this, and I know they're going to be up for this gig.

Tents are springing up all over the place, from the main lot stretching down to the actual site, like a temporary colony. A few thousand ravers are already here, most forgoing their usual kooky rave fashion in favor of hoodies and the like, to protect themselves from the cold that inevitably descends on the California desert at night.

There's very little light, outside of the fairly meager special-effects lighting, and most of the cars are too far away for their headlamps to have much effect. Because of this lack of light pollution, the crystal clear black skies bring forth the dazzling sight of a billion stars, stretching like a jeweled blanket from horizon to horizon. It's something you won't find in any city, anywhere. When standing at a distance away from the party, it's almost like being on the moon or maybe Mars. It makes one feel very small, and very fortunate to be there in that special place.

(Of course, you also really have to be careful not to step on a rattlesnake out there in the dark!)

The main stage stands in a basin at the foot of a large vertical rock wall that looks to be a couple of hundred feet high. A mammoth 30-foot blow-up alien looms over everything from the back, while the huge yellow Tonka sound system blasts the music right through the packed crowd and across the desert sands. The people are already heavily into it. They're gulping up the atmosphere like they gulp up water out here. They're determined to have a good time, and with good reason. There is no other kind of ambiance like this to be found in any kind of conventional party. It is celebrating at its most primal and minimalist, completely removed from civilization, much like "Burning Man" used to be before the RVs overran it. It's so basic that you feel almost directly connected with the elements that make up this extreme environment you're temporarily inhabiting. You half-expect to be in the middle of a very happy "Mad Max" movie, except with turntables.

Some begin scrabbling up the rocks (not a very bright idea, to be sure), while others break out road flares, the red light creating an almost Tatooine-like ambiance in the nooks and crannies up there. I'm reminded a bit of the Doors' "Celebration Of The Lizard," in which Jim Morrison describes the gatherings of hippie desert rats in places much like this one. However, there is one major problem when you're dancing up on the rocks: What the hell else can you do? Nothing! You're stuck up there until you decide you want to go somewhere else, and then you have to climb all the way back down that wall. Smart, huh?

Christopher Lawrence goes on sometime before midnight, his tall, lanky, blond figure jutting above the decks. The crowd is jazzed to see him, as Christopher at this point has become something of a local legend, and people can sense he's on the verge of hitting the big time in this genre. His soaring progressive trance sound is ideal for this desert atmosphere, as it blends with the surroundings in a way that a lot of house music just doesn't. It makes you reach for the sky, and when you do, you almost believe that you can touch it. It's a major reason why the West Coast trance sound pioneered by him, Sandra Collins and many of the crew playing tonight has become so successful out here in California.

After a while (and several great musical peaks), the wind begins to pick up. And up. And up. And before too long, to everyone's consternation it has whipped into an honest-to-goodness sandstorm. This is way beyond simply being annoying: the sand is being blown horizontally through the air at upwards of 60 mph. It stings exposed skin like you wouldn't believe, and it's becoming nearly impossible to see more than a few feet in front of you, even with your eyes shielded. This is not a good situation.

I grab my camera gear and run for a friend's tent, along with most of the crowd that's making for the tent colony. It's a struggle to push myself through the seemingly living currents of sand that are flying at breakneck speed all around me. Once inside, my friend and I zip up the entrance and make sure that there are absolutely no ripped areas or holes where the sand can get in. As it turns out, we are lucky, for there are many in other, flimsier tents that are getting precious little protection from the storm... those tents that haven't been blown over, that is. Yeah, I'm pretty fortunate at the moment.

One group that's getting no protection whatsoever are the hundreds of ravers who have chosen to brave these conditions and remain in front of the stage. I honestly have no idea what's driving these kids; to me, you would have to be truly dedicated or nearly insane to want to stay out there in the blinding sand. Those are some of the bravest partiers I've seen in who knows how long.

From the inside of the tent, the sound from the stage is being intermittently obscured by the howling wind, which has been messing big time with Christopher's set. Poor guy, he doesn't have the option of ducking out! His turntable arms are being blown all over the place, in spite of the

The storm hits the party: note the sand blowing horizontally at the top of the frame. Photo: Michael Tullberg

anemic efforts of the crew to shield the decks. They come up with a rather drastic solution: they take stacks of quarters and tape them to the ends of the arms, so that they weigh down the needles enough to keep them on the records. It seems to work, so they keep going.

(Much later, I was chagrined to find out that Christopher was performing that night with a lot of acetates, which became totally grooved out and ruined thanks to the heavy needles grinding the sand into the records!)

INSERT: HELEN O'NEILL

In the desert of California, the rave "Dune 4" took place. It went down in

history, because of the music, because of the vibe, and because of the huge wind-
storm that blew through. Thee-O, Taylor, Christopher Lawrence, Garth, Doran,
Robbie Hardkiss and Bradley B were the music masters.

A month or so after, I was talking to Christopher and I asked, "Any chance
you recorded your set?"

He said, "No. I tried to clean the records I used. I took each one to the bath-
tub and soaked them, hoping to get the sand out. No luck."

It turns out he was only able to replace half those records.

So to all of us on that dance floor, even though that set is lost in the wind, we
carry those tunes, that vibration with us, forever.

After a long while—I have no idea exactly how long—the wind finally
begins to die down. Slowly, people begin to emerge from their tents, looking around and testing the air to see if they'll have to scurry back inside.
They're finding that the storm has covered practically everything with a
layer of sand and dust. It's going to take more than a little shaking to get
it all off.

Robbie Hardkiss has taken over for Christopher, and he shifts the
returning crowd into a higher gear. It must be around 4:00 AM or so, so
Robby's set begins in darkness and lasts into the pre-dawn. People are
happy to be out of the tents and back on the dance floor (er, dirt), and
the energy is beginning to rise once again. Robbie's sound isn't like Christopher's epic trance arias; it's earthier, more grounded, but no less festive.
And funnily enough, nobody's complaining.

Eventually, inexorably, the sun comes up. In the desert, it's absolutely
beautiful; nature's color palette is on full display as the familiar yellow ball
climbs above the horizon. There's no way any of my pictures can do it

justice, so I instead focus on Doran, who's taken to the decks somewhere around 6:00 or so to restart the trance marathon. Now the crowd definitely has found its second wind as daylight breaks over the site. Everyone is happy again and they're determined to get as much fun out of this as they can, for they know that after 10:00 AM, the temperature here is going to rise dramatically.

One of the more flamboyant local rave impresarios (who I'll call Haley) is riding around on someone's shoulders. She's wearing a clear plastic mini-dress and nothing else, meaning you can see everything…and I mean everything. Well, that's Haley for you—definitely not afraid to show herself off. I notice that she's not the only one, either, as a couple of other girls have decided to go topless. Nothing compared to the legions of EDM girls who today hit parties in pasties and little else, but still eye-catching.

It's just amazing that all these people are managing to have such a good time after having to endure such an ordeal. It's one thing to be inconvenienced by delays in a standard concert situation, but what happened out here was potentially hazardous. For the dancers that remained out in that storm, it was like the honing of a sword. A trial by fire. And to see the smiles on their faces as they jump and cavort now…it's just short of mind-blowing. The fact that pretty much everyone is chipper again is a real testament to the transformative power of the music, this place, and the rave scene. It's something to marvel at, and to be proud of.

Even so, I'm exhausted and I've still got a four-hour trip back to L.A. in front of me. With the heat rising, it's definitely time to bail.

Getting out proves not to be a problem, but I was right: it's a nail-biter getting to the gas station. I'm literally running on fumes before gratefully crawling up the ramp to the gas pumps that appear like an oasis by the side of the road. Intense relief…and now I can finally really relax and think upon what just happened last night. And smile.

21 JIVANA (RAVER J) ('95)

JIVANA (Raver J) is a raver, a hooper, an author, an activist and a wife. She is one of the founders of the Electronic Music Alliance.

I'm not sure how many parties I had been to prior to the one I am about to tell you about, but I, like so many of us, was hooked from the beginning. My first "rave" was a Spiritworld production in Las Vegas: their annual Pimp and Ho ball. It was an "adult" rave in that it was 21+ and, at the time, of much more scandalous attire than what was found at regular parties. Now, of course, that sexualized attire is almost commonplace.

That first party was amazing, as our first times mostly are. The next event was even better. This was, what I would consider at the time more of a true rave, though I still recognized it being a commercial endeavor. It was Together as One, New Year's Eve, at the Los Angeles Coliseum. Walking into the arena blew my mind. The creativity of the individuals, the energy of all the people…and the vibe was not as overtly sexual as my first party; it was childlike, playful. Energy swirled around the arena so beautifully in that space. I felt like I had found my tribe, one of 50,000 new people. World changing.

These events were pivotal for me. Another would be watching The Crystal Method for the first time in San Diego at a venue called 4th and B. I was familiar with their music from working at a strip club, because the girls there always had the best taste in music. I remember I went with one of my colleagues. I'm not sure if the band started with "Keep Hope Alive" or not (it was for their "Tweekend" tour), but I could not believe the sounds coming out of their synthesizers. Back then, I swear there was nothing else that sounded like them, especially when they played live like that. That's how it felt anyway, as I melted into their groove...astral and inter-dimensional.

But it would be at another Spiritworld party, in Vegas again, Summer of Love circa 2002 or 2003, where I would have a truly religious experience. I think this story will lend evidence that you don't need to be at a spiritually based event to have an awakening. Through our culture, it can be as spontaneous as it was for me.

I was on the floor of the mainstage, toward the back area where you can dance with flow toys or use your arms and legs for any large movements. Something for everyone in that quasi-zone—it's where breakdancers live and the personal light shows happen. It's also sometimes where the bar will be, and so it was that night, where my crew had emerged from the crowd to make a pit stop on the way out.

As my friends went to the bar to get drinks, I stayed to dance. I don't know who was on. It could have been Paul Oakenfold or it could have been Spiritworld DJ resident, Beej...I was just having fun, getting my last dancing in before we went up to a room for an after-party. My platinum blonde hair had been tucked into a long, glowing, tangerine wig that night.

I had matching rhinestone-encrusted glasses, and a psychedelic sun-ray swirl mesh bell-bottom outfit. I was orange sunshine. As I do, I had my eyes closed as I danced in the rain of sound with my slick, white, platform go-go boots on.

Jivana (Raver J) – Photo: Michael Tullberg

There was nothing I did in particular that night, and I honestly don't think it was the track I was listening to, as I believe all of our music can be this potent. I think it was just my time to receive an experience like this.

We were in an indoor arena, but it was as if the skies had parted and the blinding sparkle of a celestial liquid honey light poured down upon my being. It was at a breakdown in the music, and so I had my arms raised anyway, as I often do, to receive that type of a moment. But this time, I would be coated in a viscous cascade of ethereal bliss. Like mini-orgasms, every cell of my body became alive as it worked its way down my body. Losing awareness of where I was, I felt like I was nearing a climactic orgasm as the alchemical music and light experience dipped below my navel. Just as I thought I might lose consciousness of my body completely and either be launched into the cosmos or dissolve into the world around me forever, my companion grabbed my hand and pulled me away out of that portal to molasses ecstasy that I was being sucked into.

Back in the normal dimension, I was, of course, a little disappointed I could not finish out the experience…but who knows where that would have taken me? Perhaps I would have burst into flames or dematerialized, only to reappear in another world where I could not share this story. I'm sure I still skipped out of that party in a light-stepped, cotton-candy twinkle daze.

I'm not sure if I made a big deal about it to anyone immediately after. We all have those experiences, don't we? That's why we love our scene. Reflecting back on that night a couple of years later, I would realize that experience had changed the trajectory of my life forever. It may have changed my DNA ;)

My consciousness becoming Consciousness, one with the Heart of the Universe. Beyond the world, beyond all dimension. All: the emanation of and the Void at once.

Years later, after going through a severe hardship, I would revisit that night in my mind and ask what that was, as I had never before and would never again feel anything quite as intense. And trust me, I have been partying now for a long time. Through research I would discover that what I experienced would be considered a bona-fide spiritual experience, just as any saint or prophet may have claimed to have had in the past. I also uncovered through my research many people in our scene reporting such experiences. I had always thought such things were for the special few, unattainable to most. This moment in my life made me realize that idea of exclusivity was incorrect. This experience is not only available to us all, but can be elicited without that environment or any consciousness-altering substances. You see, partying would one day lead me to yoga, which would lead me to an event where I would have a very similar, but again, not as intense experience.

So I am sharing my tale, because I want everyone to know that if you have ever felt this, then you are, I hope, now validated. If you have not experienced something quite as profound as this, please know it is available to you. Keep dancing.

I think it is important in this day and age to realize that what we are experiencing collectively as a culture is a spiritual thing. That feeling of being unified with a few, a few hundred, or tens or even hundreds of thousands of people is real. The energy most certainly is. On some level, it changes us no matter what. Now, I used to believe that it changed us all for the better. From being in the scene long enough now, I see that it is not always so. We can fall back into unproductive old habits. Love is a practice. The energy we have access to is a potential. We can choose to recycle it back into our parties only, or we can utilize that potential and choose to channel some of it back into our world for the greater good. As an activist or art activist—a.k.a. artivist—it is my experience that we need a balance of both. We need our parties to recharge us, but we should not lose sight of its real beauty, which is giving us real access to the energy of love that can transform the world. As we know, the planet needs and will continue to need a lot of TLC. The love we cultivate on the dance floor can be shared - so dance on, my lovely ravers. Awaken and share your love with the world.

22 HELEN O'NEILL - LOTUS L.A. RECAP ('99)

Helen O'Neill has been a retail entrepreneur, magazine editor, photographer, and all-around raving veteran.

(Originally written for Lotus magazine, reprinted with permission by the author)

New venues, new clubs and old clubs reviving have made the start of '99 fresh and new. Anniversaries and birthday celebrations have reminded us that after all the trials and errors, we're still hanging in there.

Aquarium celebrated its second anniversary with the house vibes of Terry Francis and Gene Ferris. The new venue in Pomona was an old '50s theater, multi-level space with cushy seats.

Club Soda had their first birthday amid stage sets, with tall tubes of light and panels of a futurist city. Brilliant lasers and visuals, which have been strangely absent from the scene, made a welcome comeback. This was a case of not realizing how much you missed something 'till it was gone. Chelsea commanded the main floor with a straight-on trance set, followed by Charlie Brown's psychedelic infused tunes. Omicron kept dancers warm outside with a lovely progressive set.

Another happy One Year Anniversary went out to speed garage's home, BUMP. Club kid extraordinaire Boom Boom's B-day brought us "Another Bitch". Ron D. Core went off with a rare set of old school acid house complete with vocals. People raved about Mike Fix and his keyboards. The hip-hop tent was hopping with SDF-1 and DJ Sonic's happy hardcore.

The author in a fun place. Photo: unknown.

Other old-timers Logic and RaveOlympia presented Universe. Dave Ralph, Taylor and Mark Lewis were on the decks with deep to progressive house. It was like a LOGIC reunion with a lot of the old regulars. Speaking of the sorely missed LOGIC, ICU has taken back its home the West End, to put on Deluxe each Sunday night. Opening night featured Kimball Collins and Sharam Jay from Germany.

For the drum & bass scene, Rewind delivered its second installment. R.A.W. and C.R.S. cooked the 2x4's and Dieselboy blasted.

The weeklies have been holding their own and there have been less busts in the rave circuit, but it's the psychedelic trance crowd that has been putting forth the major efforts with décor and talent. New crew Energia Magica brought in S.U.N. Project, from Germany. Yes, it has happened. If house is disco, then trance is heavy metal and these guys completed the circle. Lead guitar with heavy licks had the dance floor moving.

Sixth Sense, the people that put on great gigs with really weird names brought out—ready?—The Electric Psychedelic Pussycat Swingers Club. The many rooms each had their own feel with different paintings and lights. One room was completely black (and very popular). Mis-evening dancers were surprised with an abstract dance shot from the Science Professor, featuring a dancer bangles in fluoro-paper, body-flirting with an evil stilted wing-clad predator. There was also a fire-breather, in case you got bored. After everyone's sense of reality had been stolen, the mind-bending continued with the hard psy-trance of DJs Jon Marc, Kavandi and Christian. Loved the Sangria.

Another newcomer, Foreign Substance, brought over psy-trancers Xerox and Freeman, from Israel. This was another event where the organizers paid attention to décor, surrounding the cement warehouse with festive banners.

Keeping with my decorations tiff, Winterfresh got the theme down right. As it was held inside an ice rink, the cold air made ravers keep their jackets on all night. Ice-skating to house and trance was balanced with the option of playing laser tag to jungle.

So all this sounds good, but maybe too good. There have been gigs on the same night every weekend that appeal to similar crowds, thus splitting the scene. It's sad to see a lot of effort put forth on a gig that is sparsely attended. The quality of events has risen, but the quantity seems too high.

The medium-sized events seem to have been having the roughest time getting the capacities they need. The small events (under 300) are based on close-knit friends, and the large ones...well, everyone loves a massive. Go Ventures' California Collective had a happy full house of 2,500. But, I'll take this complaint any day over last season's rash of shutdowns. And the new creative efforts have put life back into the scene.

I leave you a little piece off my favorite flyer from newcomers Fuzzy Fridays. (Price info: $10 all night if you wear something fuzzy, $12 if you have exact change, $15 otherwise)

-helen13

23 SABRINA DOLLING - RAVING SAVED MY LIFE ('00)

Sabrina Dolling is a raver, manager, Burner and survivor.

In the dark, nurturing, warehouse womb of an underground culture, I found something deep within my soul that has forever changed my view of the world and undoubtedly saved my life.

As a child, I had only ever experienced abuse, tragedy, and dysfunction. I was moved around from state to state until settling into the San Francisco Bay area when I was seven. My one bit of refuge was an old grey Walkman with giant black buttons and a rigid tuning wheel. I was obsessed with listening to music. I would hide from the world by climbing a tall tree and cradling myself in its branches while scanning the radio stations. One night in 1994, when I was just eight years old, I heard a sound that I had never heard before and I was instantly captivated. It sounded electric and fast paced. My body just wanted to move and I felt happy.

Back then on Saturday nights in San Francisco, DJ Aaron Axelsen used to host "Subsonic Underground," a nonstop mix of electronic music from midnight until 3:00 AM. I would anxiously wait every week to hear these amazing sounds and hit the "record" button on my Walkman. I remember dancing around with glow-in-the-dark nail polish, twirling and jumping to the synthetic sounds that were swimming in my little ears. A couple of songs that first captured my love for electronic music were a trance remix of "Spin Spin Sugar" by the Sneaker Pimps, "I'll Fly With You" remixed by DJ Gianni, "Around The World" and "Da Funk" by Daft Punk, and "Groove is In The Heart" by Deee-Lite. However, during the peak of my raving experience, a couple of influential songs were "Halcyon On and On" by Orbital, "Heaven Scent" By John Digweed, and "Children (Future Breeze)" by 4 Clubbers.

Because of my traumatic childhood, I had a really hard time growing up. I was incapable of making friends in school, was constantly bullied and picked on, and had no sense of belonging. As I grew into a teenager, I felt like there was no point to life. I didn't want to be a part of this sick world and was extremely self-destructive and suicidal.

One night when I was fourteen, sporting baggy jeans and a neon tank top, a group of older kids said that I looked like a raver. "What's a raver?!" I asked. They explained to me that a rave was essentially a concert for electronic dance music where everyone wears bright colors and dances all night. I told them how much I loved electronic music and how that was pretty much all I listened to. They decided they were going to take me to my first rave.

The event was Cyberfest 2001, a massive held in South San Francisco. The day before the rave, my friends helped me get dressed. We picked out a pair of neon-blue parachute pants, an Atari tank top, and purple KangaRoos shoes. I remember having butterflies in my stomach on the way there, having no clue what to expect, but having faith nonetheless. I loved electronic music and trusted the people I was with.

As we were waiting in line outside of the venue, I was enamored with everyone's outfits. So many colors and patterns, fuzzy fabrics, stuffed animals, glitter, and neon! Everyone was wearing kandi bracelets. You could hear the muffled beat pulsating from inside, a nonstop rhythmic *boom-boom-boom-boom*. The air smelled like clove cigarettes and Vicks VapoRub.

We eventually made it through the doors and down a long stretch of hallway, where people I'd never met gave me hugs and I was gifted my first kandi bracelets (which I still own to this day). My friends made a meeting point near a water fountain where we were to meet at if anyone got lost or separated—these were pre-cellphone days. We finally made our way to the main dance floor, where the energy was larger than life and the music was so loud, you could feel it vibrating in your chest. It was packed with bodies, but it felt safe, like we all somehow knew each other. People were dancing with glow sticks, jumping up and down, yelling with their hands in the air, and having fun like nothing I'd ever seen. I remember a feeling washing over me that told me I was exactly where I was supposed to be.

What happened inside that event forever changed the trajectory of my life. A whole new world was opened to me. For the FIRST TIME in my entire life, I felt ACCEPTANCE by my peers, by complete strangers. Everyone was smiling, hugging me and giving me high fives as I walked down the hallways. I felt love in my heart, a feeling I wasn't used to. I HAD FOUND MY PEOPLE. I had a reason to love and to give. I decided right then and there that I wanted to live. I was a raver.

At one point, I rolled my ankle in the middle of the dance floor. A whole group of people helped me up and made sure I was okay, showing me how to stretch and work through the pain so I could dance more. It was a community of people who cared about each other and looked out for one another. We were all brothers and sisters.

That night, I felt endorphins I didn't know I had, experienced feelings I didn't know were possible, and made lifelong friendships. I now had a healthy way to release all of the stresses of life. Once you realize that you are capable of feeling love and happiness, you know you can feel them again and you start to strengthen those synapses. You live knowing that happiness *is* possible.

That was my beginning. Little did I know how much more there was to come.

2007 was one of the most memorable years for me in all of my raving history, for two of the most influential memories I have happened that year. The first was when I went to an outdoor renegade party in Sacramento with my best friend. While we were getting ready at her house, I put on my then-favorite song, "Groove Jet" by Spiller. I told her that in the countless raves I had been to at that point, I had never heard this song at one of them, and that I would probably lose my mind if I did hear it. Fast forward to that evening: the two of us were sitting in the grass, not very impressed with the music that was playing. I asked her if I should go up and ask someone who was next, and she said that would be the equivalent of criticizing a painter's art, so I decided against it. As we were talking, I heard the background beat of my favorite song getting mixed in. I jumped up and yelled "THAT'S MY SONG!!" My girlfriend told me that I was just hearing things. Seconds later, it mixed full-blown into my song and I ran straight to the front of the decks, yelling back to my friend, "I'LL SEE YOU ON THE DANCE FLOOR!"

When I got up to the decks, I looked up and saw one of my all-time favorite DJs, Eric Barlow. I had every demo CD he'd made at that point, but had only seen him spin once before. I was ecstatic and couldn't control myself. I danced so hard that a small group of people circled around me to

The author (R), Eric Barlow and friend. Photo unknown.

watch as I sung every word to the song. At the end of the song, I looked up, and Eric handed me the record from behind the decks, autographed with his name. It is still one of my most prized possessions. After his set, I walked up to him and thanked him, and ended up helping him carry his records and equipment to his car. He gifted me a copy of a record that he produced, and my girlfriend and I hung out with him and his friends until the morning light.

My second favorite moment, and the most life-affirming encounter I've ever experienced, was when I had the opportunity to sit with my all-time favorite DJ, DJ Dan. It was after Love Fest in San Francisco, where

Dan played an amazing set at one of the main soundstages at the parade. I decided to go to this event solo and let the universe bring me to who I was supposed to be with. I ended up running into one of my best friends that I had met back at my first rave in the middle of the dance floor, while Dan was spinning.

After the event, my friend and I decided to go to The End Up, our favorite after-hours club in the city. We danced until dawn and I'm so glad we did. As the sun was coming up and sunglasses were coming on, I decided to take a break from dancing and headed to the outdoor patio, where I spotted DJ Dan sitting with Donald Glaude up in the outdoor loft. I gathered up my courage and walked over to Dan, gave him a hug, and told him that he was the most influential DJ in my life. He was so receptive to the compliment and thanked me in turn. I sat next to him and talked for over an hour about how powerful his music is and how it can brighten even the darkest of days. He told me that is why he creates it, to bring happiness into people's lives, because that's what it did for him. I told him about how music had brought me out of my depression and saved my life, and he understood and reciprocated the love and passion.

I have learned so much from the hundreds of raves that I've participated in over the last decade and a half. I've learned how to drive well and follow obscure directions to hard-to-find places (pre-GPS days). I've learned to trust people, my instincts, and open my heart. I've learned yoga and meditation within my community. I've learned how to give and receive. I've learned gratitude, love, and appreciation. I've learned how to dance all night and how to take care of my body. I've learned how to help people when they are down, and how to love myself. I've also learned how to give great hugs, high fives, and massages. But most of all, I've learned how to live.

Today, I work and volunteer for countless festivals including Burning Man, Lucidity, NNMF, and Enchanted Forest. This will be my ninth consecutive year with Burning Man and my third year in a management position with them. I do set up, tear down, conflict resolution, and generally help anyone that needs a hand or is having a bad experience. I do everything I can to support the community and share the love.

THANK YOU!!!

24 JOSH GLAZER - MOTOR ('00)

Joshua Glazer is an editor whose history in the electronic music world includes Editor-At-Large for THUMP, magazine editor at URB, DJ, and promoter at the Detroit dance club Motor.

The Wednesday before Thanksgiving is always a HUGE night for Detroit bars and clubs, with all of the city's expats back in town eager to meet up with old friends and get shit-faced, before spending the next day trapped with their families.

The first major party I ever promoted with my partner Jon Ozias was on Thanksgiving Eve of 1998. We had recently come back from a trip to New York, where we had attended the Concrete Jungle party and become fascinated with the drum and bass scene. Detroit didn't have any D&B parties that we knew of, so we went to Motor-Detroit, the city's preeminent techno venue, and convinced them to let us take over the second room and book two local techno DJs, Paris and Punisher, to play D&B all night long. The fact that Frankie Bones was headlining in the main room that night meant the club would be packed no matter what. With nothing to lose, they gave us a shot, and we impressed them by building a custom

DJ booth that was meant to look like a post-apocalyptic scene from an anime movie. We even wrote the words "Take Cover" in Japanese on a piece of fiberboard painted to look like decayed metal and hung it over the DJs. It wasn't much, but the extra effort impressed the owner enough to let us do more events, which eventually led to Jon and me taking over the booking and promotions duties for the club full-time.

By Thanksgiving of 2000, Jon and I had been promoting at Motor for two years and we had things down pretty cold. That year, we booked a special night featuring Detroit techno innovators CKDK (Carl Craig, Kevin Saunderson, Derrick May and Kenny Larkin) for a party called "Blueprint." For decorations that year, we decided to wallpaper the club in actual blueprints—easy. More complicated was that Derrick and Kevin wanted to do a four-turntable tag-team performance. There was no room to set up four turntables in the small corner DJ booth, so we had to set them up on the raised VIP seating area. Most clubs would have just dragged in some card tables for this one night, but Motor owner Dan Sordyl had a better idea. We decided to permanently move the DJ booth to this new location, which meant running two 9-inch-wide by 20-foot-long metal pipes through the stage floor, through the concrete floor underneath, down into the basement, and into the concrete foundation of the building.

Setting up the new booth took about two days of seriously heavy construction that was only finished an hour or so before the club opened. In the meantime, Jon and I had other concerns. In addition to the party at Motor, we had partnered up with local concert promoters Ritual to produce a Paul Oakenfold show on the very same night, several miles away at St. Andrews Hall. We woke up that Wednesday morning with not one but

TWO parties to throw.

My schedule was planned out to the minute: Wake up early and go pick up the new club flyers from Klever Printing. Then go across the Canadian border to Windsor to pick up a bunch of old blueprints from our architect friend, Dennis Buj. Finally, drive back to Motor and hang the blueprints all over the club. Jon, in the meantime, had to make not one, not two, but THREE trips to the airport that day, since Oakenfold, his opener D:Fuse, and his manager were all flying in at different times.

I made it to Klever with no problems and was even running early enough to stop across the street to grab a coffee at a new cafe/tattoo shop run by Eric Vato, who was also a party photographer for Real Detroit Weekly and a Detroit police officer. But when I left the cafe, disaster struck. I went to my car, only to discover that I had parked illegally and was given the dreaded "boot." The only way to get it off was to go to the parking office about ten blocks away and pay the fine. It was a little after 11AM and the office was closed from noon until 1:30 for lunch. I sprinted across downtown Detroit, getting there with minutes to spare.

The fine was $300, pretty much all the money I had in the world. The office only took checks and cash, no credit cards. The woman at the counter told me there was an ATM across the street, so I raced over, desperate to get this handled before they took their lunch break. I got to the ATM only to discover that it had a $200 maximum on withdrawals (this was Detroit, people). I ran back over as the clerk was locking the doors.

"The ATM only gives out $200," I told the woman.

"I know," she replied.

"Why didn't you tell me that?" I growled back.

"You didn't ask," she shrugged and locked the door.

At this point, Jon was on his way back from the first of three airport runs. I called him and begged him to bring me $100 so that I could get my car back. He dropped off the first DJ at the hotel and hustled over to the parking office to deliver me cash. In the meantime, knowing that I was now running several hours late, I began to call a bunch of friends to come to Motor and help hang the blueprints that I still had to pick up in Windsor. As always, when things got tight, our friends were there to bail us out and make the party happen.

I finally got my car de-booted and headed across the border to pick up the blueprints. Mercifully, this went off without any more complications and I was back at Motor by around 6PM, three hours before opening. With our friends' help, we got the blueprints hung. The new flyers were placed on the tables and taped up in the bathrooms. In the meantime, Jon had finished with his DJ pickups, and we agreed to meet at St. Andrews Hall to make sure everything was squared away for Oakenfold.

People were already starting to arrive as we got there, but everything seemed fine. D:Fuse was on the decks and Oakie was settled in backstage. Being the techno fans we were, Jon and I both wanted to be at Motor, so we recruited local DJ and promoter Hugh Cleal to take care of Oakenfold while we went to see our Detroit boys.

By the time we got back to Motor, it was midnight and Kenny was finishing his opening set in the main room, while Carl was playing cool experimental stuff in the lounge. We cracked open our first beers and laughed at how crazy the day had been. The club was seething with energy as Derrick and Kevin stepped up to the decks. They had never played to-

THE RAVER STORIES PROJECT 171

gether on four turntables before, but soon found their groove as the crowd went wild.

Around 1AM, I found myself down in our basement office, shooting the shit with Mike (Foton) Fotias, whose Burst sound company ran the new sound system Motor had recently installed, while the room rattled from the bass kicking upstairs.

That's when the lights went out. Then on. Then out again.

Foton lept up and ran to the amplifier closet (sudden power surges are not generally good for expensive amps and processors). I made my way up to the main room, grappling in the dark when the power went out again. By the time I got upstairs, the sold-out crowd was standing still in utter confusion. The Intelli-beams on the ceiling flickered meekly and the electricity fluxed up and down.

As I stood there frozen, one of the security guards grabbed me and dragged me to the back door that led into the alley behind the club. A car had crashed into a utility pole halfway down the block. The transformer hanging at the top had exploded, raining sparks down onto the street while the lights on the whole block flickered on and off.

I made my way up to the DJ booth and quieted down the 1000+ drunk, scared and angry people standing there. "The transformer up the street blew," I shouted. "Party is over. Sorry everyone. And, oh yeah, stay out of the back alley!"

We emptied the club, staff and all, killed the main power supply in the basement to stop the surges, and locked the doors behind us. Next, we headed back down to St. Andrews where Oakenfold was finishing up his set at 2:00 AM. We found our way backstage and told everyone the story as their jaws dropped to the floor. As always, somebody suggested an after-hours, but it was late and we had family to tend to the next day.

Hours later, as I sat at Thanksgiving dinner with my parents and brother, recounting the adventures of the previous night, I had only one thing on my mind. "I hope they fixed the power," I told them. "We have another party to throw tomorrow."

The author, spinning in 2008. Photo: Michael Tullberg

25 JASON DEYARMIN - JUJUBEATS ('09)

Jason Deyarmin has been spinning in southern California as DJ Jason Splat for the past twenty years.

"How I met my Sonic Soulmate in a Bumble Bee Love Swarm"

The year was 2009. The party was the JujuBeats festival at the beautiful Lake Irvine.

I had been to the lake before; I'd had the good fortune to spin at JujuBeats 2008 the year prior, which was an epic party and a huge DJ gig for me. Up to that point, I had made a career out of playing smaller, more intimate shows. JujuBeats '08 was the biggest stage and sound system I had played on to date, and I had an absolute blast spinning there! But on a more personal note, as the summer sun set on my gig that day, it was also setting on a long relationship I had been in. So for me, JujuBeats '08 was kind of bittersweet. I ended up being single for a long, lonely stretch afterwards; a role I was unfamiliar with as a serial monogamist. I was still fairly active in the underground scene getting frequent bookings, but now I was flying solo to the parties and clubs.

My solitary streak went on for the better part of a year—until I ran into a new lady friend. We met at a chance encounter at the Monday Social club in Hollywood. It turned out that she was also a fairly active DJ, on the drum and bass side of the scene. Her DJ name was Daemia, which is a reference to a dark and badass female character from a famous video game. The name suited her musical style, which was also dark and badass.

We went out a few times and were hitting it off. Then one day, we realized we were both on the lineup for the JujuBeats '09 summertime festival. Though we had just recently met, we agreed to go there together, carpool and even camp in the same tent together. Days went by and the date finally arrived: August 1st, 2009. We met at my place in Long Beach, packed up my Mountaineer with all of our gear, and headed out to the festival.

The drive down to Lake Irvine wasn't bad...maybe because we left during the day. We both had afternoon sets on different stages; she was spinning in the "Flower Power Garden" Dnb/Dubstep & Glitch stage, and I was on the "Bumble Bee Love Swarm" Progressive/Funky House stage. Our time slots overlapped for about thirty minutes, so it was going to be tricky for us to support each other's sets. Nonetheless, we were both up for the challenge; we would make it work.

We made it in to the camping area, which was already surprisingly packed, and set up our tent near the lake. We stopped briefly to talk to some friends, but we were on a mission to make it to our sets on time, which were fast approaching. Luckily, we spotted the main promoter driving by on a golf cart and he offered to drive us to our stages. There's something profound about travelling around these big festivals on a cart. This was a big help in getting us to our sets in time.

We arrived to Daemia's stage first: The Flower Power Garden. This stage would also host Bassnectar, The Glitch Mob, Z-Trip and 6-Blocc. She was scheduled to spin in the late afternoon, going on half an hour before me. Daemia set up and promptly began to cut into the lazy afternoon haze with some up-front underground drum and bass tunes. This was one of the first times I heard her spin live and I was impressed!

I danced on Daemia's stage for about thirty minutes, then I had to jam over to my stage for my set, which was directly across the field—a long walk, but within eyeshot. I gave her a kiss and was on my way. I made it there just in time and got right on the decks. As I was spinning, it was surreal to look across the fields and see Daemia also playing in the distance. We were smiling and waving at each other while simultaneously spinning on different stages!

About halfway into my set, the twilight began to fall and the field filled up with people. Daemia made it over after she'd finished and joined me on stage for the rest of my time. I got to drop one of my favorite tracks, which was a Bob Marley/house remix, just as the sun was setting on about a thousand friends and ravers. Getting to play on this massive stage that would later host DJ Dan and Donald Glaude, two of my all-time favorite DJs, was a sublime moment and a high point of my career.

The rest of my set was like a dream...the tracks seemed to play themselves, coming organically to the decks. The DJs and friends that said hi to me while I was spinning were awesome; I am very grateful for their support. I finished my set and packed up my gear. Then, Daemia and I proceeded to head down into the party itself. It was a fantastic event. We bounced around from stage to stage, catching some epic DJ sets and running into close friends. One of her closest friends was there and happy to see our blossoming romance. She whispered a word of caution to me: "If you break her heart, I'll kick your ass." That was intense. (Needless to say, no asses have been kicked to this day!)

We frolicked on through this dreamy night together, wandering through the lush fields and trees in this raver's paradise. At dawn, we made it back to our tent for some alone time. Eventually, we fell asleep in the tent for what must have been a long time. I say that because when I woke and unzipped the tent to look outside, it was the middle of the next day and nearly everyone was gone! We were the last people there; not another tent was in sight. We laid there together, basking in the aftermath of this epic adventure, enjoying our company and the silence for a while longer, before a guy in a truck drove over and told us to pack it up.

Truth be told, in a sense we never really left that tent. Daemia and I continued to date after that, and eventually started spinning together. We went on to DJ around the country, then we moved in together and got engaged. And years later, we got married in early August, right around the same time as that JujuBeats event. We have been married for over four years now, and celebrate our anniversary each year on August 1st. I truly think that amazing night at JujuBeats '09, where we scrambled to support each other's sets and had an amazing campout excursion under the stars together, played a big part in solidifying our cosmic connection. Thank you, JujuBeats, for bringing me my sonic soulmate in a bumble bee love swarm!

26 ONNOLEIGH SWEETMAN - BURNING MAN ('11)

Onnoleigh Sweetman is a dancer, raver, writer, part-time unicorn, and the founder of Nytronix Entertainment and The Studio Nytronix in Las Vegas, Nevada.

"Journey of Fire Part 2"

"From the dust we came and to the dust we shall return and emerge new beings of light." —Onnoleigh Sweetman

I prefer to call Burning Man "Utopia"; a sort of magical place where the misfits and madmen go.

A place where people of all kinds come to play, build, dance, burn and most importantly, renew. An almost-fifteen-year veteran of Burning Man, I find every year to be a pertinent lesson in many areas of artistic and spiritual development. Each year, the playa has graciously and not so graciously handed me a stern lesson in detachment. Not surprising coming from an event whose artists and performers spend nearly an entire year in preparation, only to burn most of the art and leave the desert with no trace of human existence at all. The playa (as most burners call it) has a way of downright kicking your ass at any sign of forced control, but will bless you in all its glory once you surrender within the dust. This has been evident every time I have gone searching for someone or something, given up, and then less than a minute later, been handed exactly what I originally was searching for on a dusty silver platter or electro thumping art car.

But behind this magical place and Utopic society, there must always be a mass intent for the gathering of the tribes. A reason for co-creation, to provoke emotion and to stir up the organized chaos. Every year, countless burners, performers, DJs, artists, sculptors and participants will explore a yearly theme through all types of media and art. The vision? As burning-man.org states, "To remove us from the context and the cares of daily life, confront us with our vital need to be, and then return us to the fellowship of a society."

And at Burning Man, you can do just that. With no cell-phone service, no television, and no Internet, it is a perfect opportunity to deprogram oneself from social media and the digital age.

But take heed: With extreme temperatures during the day, hour-long white-outs and equally extreme temperatures at night, there is a survival guide. It details what it takes to survive a week with no running water and no corporate stands to purchase things from. And with the Ten Principles solidly in place, values like radical self-expression and radical self-reliance become terms of endearment. Burning Man isn't for the weak of heart; instead, I see it existing for those who are restless at heart. Most of these burners are restless with the mundane life of the 9-to-5 job, restless with the mediocre, and restless with conformity. It takes a diehard to rough it in a tent for a week and a downright warrior to spend two to three weeks setting up camp only to tear it down or burn it, and start over again for next year.

The author at Burning Man. Photo unknown.

2011: The day of exodus to the burn was upon me, and for the first time, I actually slept the night before leaving. Refreshed and ready to go, I stood proudly as it seemed this year I had the preparation dialed in. Everything was packed neatly in Ziploc bags to avoid the ravenous dust that was soon to be upon me, my ultimate Burning Man list was checked from top to bottom, and my spirit was calm and centered. Having my ass kicked a thousand times over by the playa in the past, this year I bowed in karmic humility, took everything that I had learned in previous years, and applied it fervently to the spiritual preparation and every other aspect of the Burning Man experience. So far, I was off to a beautiful start.

At 5:00 PM on Saturday, I met my rideshare at the RV rental place. Jeremy, a dance producer, and Jon, a 26-year-old, were both from Camp Auto Sub in Boston, Massachusetts, and both virgin burners. The excitement was in the air and I remember looking back at my first burn, thinking how nothing could ever prepare these two for the magic they were about to experience, and how in one week, we would all step back into this RV, forever changed by the initiation and cleansing of the dust. One can see pictures or watch videos about Burning Man, but there is nothing in comparison to the actual live event itself. I also wondered what was in store for me. I had set myself on a diligent mission of flowing and allowing with whatever the playa had in store for me, and felt more prepared than ever to return home to the dust.

The ride was calm in spite of a little hail and lightning on the way, and Jon and I (both fans of psychedelic trance) rocked out to Shpongle and Infected Mushroom most of the way. I was surprised at how clear the roads were, as we'd seen hardly any vehicles, hippie busses or RVs on the way. This, of course, was the calm before the storm. With a 50,000-person limit set by the BLM and a two-lane highway from Fernley, Nevada all the way to Black Rock, I almost cringed at what could be a monstrous gate wait into the event. But that was still a day away. The playa had a mini-adventure in store for Jon and me, and it would be an almost 48-hour trek from start to finish to the gates of Burning Man.

At 4:00 AM, we landed outside of Reno in Lemon Valley. With an early entry pass for Jeremy, we decided to crash for a few hours at my dear friend and light worker Crisalicous' house. It had been nearly a year since we'd seen each other and I welcomed a pre-burn communion with her. After only a few hours of sleep, we were up and ready to start the next day. Jeremy's plans were to head straight to Burning Man, which meant that Jon and I needed to find a way to Fernley and the Love gas station by 8:00 PM. A few phone calls later, we ventured into Reno to designer and artist Marcio Decker's house. As with all my trips to Northern Nevada, the Sunday experience was like a family reunion for me, seeing old faces from the dearest times of my life, which mostly were encountered in Burning Man's backyard of Reno. From Marcio's, we headed over to meet the countless burners of camp EZRA, to assist in the final stages of their EZCAR-GOGO art car—a large snail with an amazing sound system. The crew was quick to assemble and then disassemble the car in preparation for its journey into the Black Rock Desert.

From Reno, Jon and I ventured into Fernley. With only my backpack, a six-gallon water jug and a zebra-print coat, I felt like a diva version of Christopher McCandless of "Into the Wild." I might not be trekking through the wilds of Alaska, but I was proud of myself for not stressing over the change of plans. Having been a producer for ten years, I normally plan, perform and execute everything that I do to a tee. This time, I decided to just trust that everything would work itself out and I would land my dancing feet on the magical dust in no time.

In Fernley, we were dropped off at a casino, where we spent the next three hours. Exhaustion started to creep in, and after a beer and dinner, I found myself almost falling asleep at a video poker machine. Sounds of a woman calling out bingo numbers beckoned annoyingly in our ears, and I couldn't help but feel anxious to get on our way. A week with no Internet, television, social media, slot machines or tourists is the highest version of a vacation for me, if there ever was one. Just pure home-grown art, with amazing people, engaging interaction and adventure. We were so close…I soon would be home…back to a place where my soul shines at its brightest and my smile at its warmest, the best version of me radiating from this physical body in all its mortal glory. We were so close. Our supplies were already on the playa and that just left one more thing: us. Our final passage into the mystical land of Burning Man!

At 9:00 PM, our final ride arrived in Fernley—TJ and Michelle, also known for the rest of the week as Mom and Dad. I had met TJ and Michelle at the 2008 burn and we'd remained stellar friends ever since. This year, they were gifting me my first-ever stay in an RV (well-deserved I might add, after roughing it in a tent for almost a decade). We loaded ourselves into the RV and were on our way. The gates were open, but as anticipated, the lines were long. We listened to BMIR radio live from the playa hosted by the Rock-star librarian, who was giving his listeners all the tips on the when and where of the week in music on the playa. The hosts were even interviewing the "Greeters". "What's your name?" I heard a man ask, and a boisterous woman replied, "Smooches!" I smiled in excitement, for "Smooches" is Elaine, one of my former performers in my first dance company, and a close friend. "We must get to her at the greeter gate!" I exclaimed excitedly, and three hours later, we did just that. I ran out of the RV to see Smooches chatting at countless burners on her loud speaker. I charged her and gave her the biggest hug possible. Nothing could be better than being greeted to the homeland of the playa with someone that has shared some of my most amazing experiences in life.

And so we were in. I had finally made it to the mother ship. We traveled the allotted speed of 5 mph and headed to 9:30 and Birthday, our home for the next week. When we arrived, "The Jellys" and the members of the "Panda Sky Bar" were working diligently on setting up our camp, which included an oversized teal bus that would be our mutant vehicle "Jelly" for the week as well. But my mission was not yet completed. It was about three in the morning on Monday and I needed to venture with Jon clear across the playa to 3:30 and Esplanade to locate Jeremy and his RV. "I'll be back before sunrise," I told my campmates, and with that, we were off.

We traveled straight ahead towards 9:30 and Esplanade, right to the Man. I was surprised at the amount of art cars and burners that were already "in it" for a Sunday night. These people apparently didn't mess around. Years before, when I first started burning, the playa would be calm and steady throughout the beginning of the week, and you could feel and see with your own eyes the energy build and grow as the days went on. The city coming into its own, ever-changing with every day, never quite looking the same. Over the past few years, with the sudden influx of people attending the event, that has changed. Monday nights have begun to feel like a Saturday with the party not missing a beat right when the sun sets...

So here I was standing directly at the base of the Man...It was 3:30 in the morning on a Monday and after my two-day hitchhiking adventure to get to this point, I reveled in my own awe and inspiration. I looked up to the wooden sculpture with gracious humility. The Man, standing tall and proud with his left leg forward, looked as though he was glancing behind him with his arms in stride, as if alluding to what he was there for. This wooden Man, in his own final passage, would soon find his way to his own destiny in the ever-so-deeply intended theme of Rites of Passage. The week would fly by and with every intent my soul could muster, I would purge everything I so badly wanted to release into this glowing structure. I looked up at this Man with a steadfast intent of soaking it all in, knowing that this too shall pass; that these moments on the playa that I crave with an unquenchable thirst would soon be a memory. In complete awareness,

I closed my eyes and took it all in: the dust beneath my feet, the sounds of electronic beats in the air, the mysticism of being in the middle of nowhere—almost as if on another planet. As I opened my eyes, I knew this was a pivotal moment for me. There was a brief time I wasn't sure I was going to make it to the event. All the preparation, all the passion, everything that I came to Burning Man for this year, was represented in that brevity of a Man; that I myself would transition along with the burning of this sculpture through my own Rites of Passage and leave the heartache from all the death that I had experienced this year behind me. In almost every sense, this wooden Man in a remote desert had become my God. My hope. My Savior…

We finally made it to 3:30 and Esplanade. None of the looking points sounded familiar and we searched diligently for Jeremy for about an hour. This is when I started to get nervous. What if we didn't find him? Could I last a few days or even a week without all my fur, costumes, and makeup? The partial glitter pony inside me decided not, and I continued to freak out some more. I had forgotten how difficult it could be at times to track a person down in a 50,000-person city. With looking points such as glowing eggs and unicorn busses, one can become consumed within the city's wonderland and become lost down its engaging rabbit hole quite easily. That's when I remembered one of my intents for the year: *"Trust the playa, let it guide you."* That's when I said, "OK playa, I give up, show me where he is now," and with that, I looked up and immediately found the RV.

Monday morning brought with it the birth of a new Utopia, and with it smiles and hugs and hellos to friends old and new. My home for the week was a two-part camp, a combination of The Jellys and The Panda

Sky Bar. The meshing of both would bring with it uplifting music that would change my point of view on compassion, camaraderie and dubstep forever.

The Jelly (a large upside down jellyfish) was being constructed by a group based out of San Francisco and Denver, Colorado. Roscoe Ferguson, who spearheaded the project, stated, "The Jelly is a 30-foot-long, two-story pleasure craft that exists for the sole purpose of creating smiles and spreading its underwater charm across the playa." A very true statement about an art car that could be described as nothing less than one of "God's motorized angels," blasting sounds that one could only refer to as dub-trance mixed with ambient music. I would witness the Jellys assemble the final stages of this labor of love for two days on the playa. The driving force behind this project? "I labor on it so that I may have the opportunity of picking up dusty strangers and friends in the desert and provide them with an amazing, unexpected experience, transportation through the hot desert sun, cold beer and water, and an elevated view to take in all that the playa has to offer," said Ferguson to me.

And speaking of views, the Panda Sky Bar made for an amazing backyard for the week. Headed up by Ashot, an engineer, this wooden structure was built on top of a school bus and stood over twelve feet tall, complete with a bar and DJ booth. Talk around the camp was that he'd put in quite a hefty sum of his own hard-earned cash to construct the bar, and that the campmates had donated $3,500 to stock the bar with liquor and cordials.

Monday also brought with it my up-close and personal introduction to the massive Funktion 1 sound system. Our direct neighbors were camp "Wide Awake," and wide awake they were, with a $200,000 art car with custom-made plexiglass covering that sound system on what looked like an antique steampunk jalopy with giant wooden wheels. This camp and vehicle had been founded by none other than the one, the only, "God of the Ravers," Pasquale Rotella. For those of you living in a forest with no contact to the outside world, Pasquale is the man responsible for the epic and mind-blowing Electric Daisy Carnival events over the past twenty years. Dark and handsome, Pasquale radiates a business charm with just the right combination of dreaminess and reserve. And here I was, camped next to the one man that has made not only a lifestyle, but a business out of his love for electronic music. Inspiration at its best.

Pasquale's camp was busy and full of energy. What looked like tour busses lined the camp one by one, and the beats coming from Wide Awake drew me in as if I were in a trance. I walked the short distance over and began my week by dancing with a refreshing smile to the DJ commanding the art car and his audience. And then it hit me—this was the camp that Las Vegas-based DJ Tatiana was camping with! I asked around the camp for Tatiana. One man asked who she was and I replied, "The Goddess of Music." With that, I made my way into the Wide Awake dome to find my goddess inside.

A tall, dark beauty with sultry, brown eyes, "Tati" stood alongside the DJ booth where numerous packages of Red Bull lined the dome, quiet in her demeanor but enriched with a calm and centered strength. One can only admit they are standing in the presence of an ancient soul when in her company. Pre-playa, we had discussed how we were going to find each other this year, and we both smiled with excitement to see one another and our RVs placed so serendipitously side by side. Tatiana, who would rock the decks the entire week with Wide Awake, had this to say: "When the music on the art car brings people from all ends of the playa seeking that sound they hear, you know you've stumbled upon all the goodness that is Wide Awake. Music moves us from the inside."

And from the inside it does. That is the driving force behind most musicians on the playa. It is, in my opinion, an example of spirit speaking to spirit—the gift we give and so graciously receive in the dusty desert of Black Rock. As I always say, "The right DJs are true musical shamans, healing their audience through the electronic beats."

The most spirited of DJs for the week, hands down, were the crew of Camp EZRA and the 60-person snail art car called the EZCAR-GOGO. With feel-good dance music at its absolute finest, the snail was headed up by lead DJ Izak Engel. Originally from South Africa, Izak had made his way to Reno nine years before and immediately found his way to Burning Man. With blonde hair and blue eyes, he exudes a sex appeal that commands the decks and the audience with such an immense, engaging energy, patrons from all over the playa were automatically drawn in to the EZCAR-GOGO. Electro house could be heard thumping all day and night from the art car, along with the boisterous community-driven dance junkies of Camp EZRA.

The Panda Sky Bar also became popular for its luscious beats as well as its day and night parties. The speakers were basically by my head while I was sleeping, and numerous times, the melodic beats pulled me from a deep slumber, where I would run up the stairs in my pjs (or barely dressed at all) ready to dance the morning away. A great backyard, if I say so myself. One morning, I recall awakening to the most delicious and ambient of sounds, and I yelled from my bunk to TJ that the music was just so damn good and we had to wake up. I made my way into my backyard and up the dusty steps to the decks of the bar, where a reserved yet commanding DJ was slaying the decks. That DJ was none other than the San Diego-based melodic genius Zak Johnson.

The sounds emanating from the speakers were a sound and style I had never heard before and it pulled me into a hypnotic state of bliss. I smiled and immediately danced right by the DJ booth. There was something mysterious and addicting about Zak. I didn't want to leave the dance floor, but instead lusted after everything that was going on behind those tables. When his set was finished, Zak lingered around the Sky Bar. That's when I approached him. "I really enjoyed watching you," I said. "I really enjoyed watching you enjoying me," he replied. From that moment on, I knew Zak J was going on my roster of top ten DJs.

As it turned out, Zak was a virgin burner who'd traveled with friends he'd mostly gone to kindergarten with. Oddly enough, somewhere in the mass of dust, there were three other burners from my old hometown in upstate New York who, as a kid, I had shared bus and bicycle rides with. One can only look back and wonder in awe remembering yourself as a child, then look to the present, amidst glowing lights and dust storms, and think how we could have ever imagined these immense illusions of grandeur we were currently experiencing. Was this predestined? That some eighteen years later, we would all be in a remote desert over 2,000 miles from our safe and conformist town nestled outside of Rochester, New York?

And that's when I came to a conclusion. I didn't go to Burning Man and become a "burner." I was a "burner" who happened to find Burning Man.

"Journey of Fire Part 3"

Amidst the lights, the music and art cars stands a structure off the grid from the party and chaos. A divine force, the very essence and the core of the festival, is truly represented in the mystical and reverent art installation known as the Temple of Transition.

Tuesday brought with it some difficult moments. My main intent for the burn of 2011 was to take my late mother's ashes and spread them at the Temple. After carrying her in my backpack for four days, the plan was to meet friends and journey to the temple that afternoon. I headed to Black Rock Syndicate, the meeting place, an hour late. As I walked the dusty path, I could almost hear my mother in my head; her excitement, awe and wonder at an event she helped me prepare for, for so many years; the special way she would say my name that only a mother could do. In my head, I explained the streets and layout of the event, the theme camps and art installations. "So here you finally are, mom," I thought to myself.

Memories of meeting a random burner named Bucket in the ICU came rushing through my head, the two of us standing outside of the hospital, thinking how our parents inside must have planned this in some serendipitous fashion. Within the first glance at each other, we knew we were both burners. There's something special about randomly meeting fellow burners in the default world. An understanding of each other that isn't spoken, it's just known.

This was it. I was really here. The thought of what I was about to do weighed heavily on my soul, and I wasn't sure if I was ready for this. Heck, I wasn't ready for her to die either, but here I was…me, expressing my ultimate fear of placing my own mother's name in the temple…

When I finally reached Syndicate, I saw longtime Reno promoter and friend, John Moon. Both Moon and another Vegas burner named JD had offered to go with me whenever I was ready. John suggested the next sunrise, but JD was already on his way there with a man he met named Prophet. And so with that, JD, Prophet and I headed to my camp for what was to be a brief detour before the journey.

Back at camp, TJ and Michelle were installing the shade structure outside our RV. Electronic beats could be heard blasting from the Panda Sky Bar, and boisterous screams and laughter from the numerous art cars passing by. I tried my best to be in the present moment, thinking, "You're at Burning Man, you're home, savor every second," but the thoughts of my mother kept weighing on my mind. It was an aching I didn't want to feel at Burning Man, but that's the thing about the burn: Everything that you carry with you, every day, presents itself head on, waiting to be recognized and to be healed. There was heaviness in my heart and I wasn't ready to step foot in that temple.

We all decided to kick back at my camp for a bit before JD and Prophet biked to the Temple. We all engaged in stellar conversations of yoga, Las Vegas swamis and more. Prophet, who had tattoos on his arm that said "THERE IS NO LIFE BUT LIFE AND WE ARE THE LIVERS," offered me a numerological card reading.

As we were chatting, a young man named Jesus from Ireland joined our conversations. He was a virgin burner and having the most profound experience. He looked at us all and, with tears in his eyes, said, "I came here to Burning Man for the party. Little did I know my mind would become expanded. I had no idea about 'spirituality' or that this existed…" I empathized completely with him, recalling my first year when I stood at the edge of Soul System at 10:00 and Esplanade to dance and welcome my first Sunday Sunrise. I remembered watching and feeling the connection between me, that desert, the sun and all the thousands of beautiful people. I didn't feel alone anymore on this journey. There were others like me. That was my first experience of "Oneness."

Some may adhere to the belief that Burning Man is just a wild party, a drunken drug fest of neo-hippies and anarchists. But there is no doubt that for those that have attended, there is a simple truth. There's a spiritual driving force about Burning Man, something that speaks to every soul. You find it walking by yourself, strolling along the dusty paths, dancing in between thousands, or trekking alone through deep playa. The meaning of existence…

"The Temple of Transition:"

Yea, though I walk through the valley of the shadow of death, I will fear no evil: for fellow Burners art with me; thy song and thy poi, they comfort me. Thou preparest a table before me in the presence of mine fears: thou anointest my head with cold water; my cup runneth over. Surely goodness and joy shall follow me all the days of my life, and I will dwell in and on the playa forever.
-Cross Sidhe

It was around 3:00 in the morning, and TJ and Michelle and I had traveled through most of the Esplanade and dance camps on our side of the playa. We were currently around 6:00 off the Esplanade, and that's when I knew that the pivotal moment was upon me. I looked to the Temple that stood in all its ephemerality a long way in the distance. I looked with a heavy heart beyond the lights, beyond the art cars, and took one slow breath. I looked to TJ and Michelle and said, "It's time." I looked ahead, and with a determination of a child to grow up and become an adult, I flipped my backpack over my shoulder. I felt like a refugee on the last legs of their journey home and knew that this would be the ultimate journey of my existence. The journey that I had so solemnly come to Burning Man to do. The journey of my own Rites of Passage: to spread my mother's ashes.

The temples of Burning Man all seem to ache with an awareness of one's own mortality. Pictures, letters and notes of loved ones that have passed line the walls. People lay their grief down in complete vulnerability to be transformed, to let go and to heal. It is a place of complete reverence, and for many years, I have found myself on my knees, sobbing out the shadows of my own soul. Memories of the year one of my closest friends, Sam Rich, who died on the playa in 2005, are always relevant when I walk through this valley of grief. Remembrance of a conversation with my mother pre-burn the year he passed. I'd looked at her and said, "Mom, it's so sad to think all of us burners will go to Burning Man and one of us might die." It was hard to wrap my head around that thought, and my mother's response was, "Onnoleigh, they die so you don't have to." Little did we know the 29 year-old man who would die later in the week would be one of my best friends, my family. I grieved hard when Sam died, and my mother was the one who comforted me, who held me amidst my screams and uncontrollable sobs. Who spoke about the afterlife the way only my mother could do.

And now I was here, in the temple again, to say goodbye to my very best friend, my mother. I wondered if Sam was there to meet her on the other side. I wondered if they shared stories, shared laughs and tears. I wondered if their spirits were watching me now or if there was a playa in another dimension for those that had transitioned.

I walked through the Temple with TJ and Michelle. We read letters of grief, poems of goodbyes and looked at pictures of happier days. We were all very quiet. We walked outside the temple facing the vast desert where echoes of thriving beats stretched out across the ancient land. I reached into my backpack and grabbed my mother's ashes.

I felt as though I was floating on top of myself and it was someone else in my body. I gently spread her ashes, feeling them become one with the dust of my most-beloved playa, my home that I had always talked about for so many years. I stood in shock as I tried to absorb what was happening. In an instant, I recalled my very first trip to the Burning Man temple in 2004 with Sam and our friends as we rode out into the void on top the USS Nevada art car. Everyone was quiet. Some were crying. The music was on silent and everyone held a demeanor of respect. It was only my second burn and I hadn't quite grasped what the temple was about. But that night, without words, I had seen it. I had felt it. The temple had become, for me, one of the most important art sculptures of Burning Man, a place where we cast aside our masks and bare the depths of our souls. And on the last night of Burning Man, the temple would be burned in silence, with thousands upon thousands of onlookers, as all of our grief reached out into the infinite skies.

Back in the here and now, Michelle and TJ stood quietly in the distance, beacons of unwavering support. There was no instantaneous release of grief for me, no great white light that healed my bleeding wounds that night. That would be a process to be continued elsewhere...

I was on my knees grasping in full fortitude that nothing last forever, and that the only thing that is everlasting is love. That's all we take with us. It transcends time, death and space. Wherever in the universe my mother was, at that very moment, I was laying aside my own mask and bleeding out into the heavens every ounce of love I have for her.

I gently arose from my knees and was met with hugs by both TJ and Michelle. The lights of the burgeoning city were rampaging with energy.

At that moment, I knew that I had cried enough for a thousand souls and a thousand deaths...and now the beats were calling me.

We began the trek back into the city, back into the chaos in search of our sound. The Man would burn on Saturday night and now we needed to live for ourselves, celebrating our own lives and dancing out the remainder of our own demons.

We happened upon an art car off the Esplanade of the city. The bass was loud and the beats were right in sync with our tastes. I took out my fire poi and lit up the night. With fire in hand, I began to ride the dark bass lines. The beats were a perfect match with my favorite time at Burning Man—the witching hour, right before the sky casts a certain color of blue and you can feel the dawn of a new day approaching. I danced it all out. Every hurt and every joy. I danced underneath the black skies and even blacker beats, where only a gathered tribe of the chosen few get to dance out the ancient wisdom, and engulf themselves in the ancient truth that is the soul-opening experience one can only find in the dust of the Black Rock Desert.

The author at the Temple Of Transition. Photo unknown.

27 GRANT GILMORE - FINDING HOME ('08)

Grant Gilmore is an electronic music journalist who is the Editor-In-Chief of EDMidentity.com.

As someone who is constantly writing about their experiences at events, the news of the scene, and more, I rarely find it hard to express my emotions in text form. I have covered events, festivals, club shows and more, all of which have brought their own unique vibe and feel with them. I attempt to analyze every moment of my journey in my efforts to provide a fair assessment of these adventures for my readers, but rarely do I ever dig deeper into my own history in the scene.

Sure, I may have been in diapers when the scene began to form in the early Nineties. I definitely missed the boat in the early 2000s, only finding my way to electronic beats from random files downloaded via Napster, Morpheus, or LimeWire. Fast forward to 2008, when I was sucked in to the electronic music scene during the initial boom of dubstep throughout North America. I couldn't get enough—it was the perfect blend of my roots in rock music, with dope beats that I could imagine hip hop artists rapping over. Hearing artists like Skream, Benga, Datsik, and Excision produce music that literally made my car shudder with excitement led me to my first event at the House of Blues in San Diego. Datsik was playing and I NEEDED to be there. It was a new world, a new place to explore, the floodgates had opened and I was floating away in bliss.

You could call it a honeymoon phase, but you'd be wrong, because that love for this scene has never left. Things have changed, people have come and gone, and yet I'm still here. Why? I do ask myself this from time to time, never really settling for one specific answer. Instead, I look to specific moments that solidified my absolute love for this community, and there are a few.

First would be the two larger events that really woke up the love inside of me. These were Abstract in 2010 and Radius in 2011, thrown here in San Diego by a now defunct company named Reset San Diego, later named Revelus. Were these events jaw dropping in production value? No, not really. What they did was bring acts who were about to be superstars, and combine that with vibes that are hard to find in the post-EDM boom world of today. Sure, there were some people that threw some negative vibes at me, but everyone was accepting of who I was. I felt that the entire show was connected, and the amount of fun I had was out of this world. At Abstract, my true "rave mom" Ashley taught me how to act at events and stay safe. Radius was the event in which I learned about PLUR in depth from my "rave dad" Dase. It was not a new term, but being able to finally understand the meaning behind it really made me question who I was before, and how I should act in the future. I wanted to become a better person, and I felt that these principles really would be a message that could change me, and maybe the whole world too.

We had a blast meeting new people and dancing away inside the Air and Space Museum, an odd venue but still was amazing in its own right. I thought it was hilarious to be inside a venue that during the day played host to schools and tourists, but at night was full of people dancing and raving away. Security did their best to control the influx of people inside the tiny entry way, and the acoustics were probably not fantastic, but just being there was awesome nonetheless. There was even a point at which Zeds Dead, who was a highlighted side stage act, had a massive crowd that forced an entire portion of the venue to be shut down.

Second, enter the behemoth Insomniac Events, and my first experience with them at Escape From Wonderland 2011. Excited to catch ATB, Steve Angello, and Afrojack, this was one of the nights that I will always remember. Attending with a different group of friends, I honestly had no idea what I was in for when I walked through security. I stuck to Kevin, one of my good friends, practically the entire night in an effort to not get swept away in the crowd. My entire world changed once again, fueling the fire inside me that told me I needed to be there. Concerts and these smaller events were cool, but being around thousands upon thousands of other people, being in the crowd and enamored by all the sights and sounds brought upon an overwhelming feeling. My friends by my side kept the comfort levels solid, and even with the minimal production at the event...I knew that this was something that was about to be much larger than I ever imagined.

When people said the world was going to end in 2012, perhaps they were partially right. Maybe one world actually did end for me, but that didn't stop another from beginning. This was the year of Swedish House

Mafia dominating the airwaves, and say what you will but the uplifting tone of their music was truly something special. This year had two events that truly stick out in my personal history as altering moments, Coachella and EDC Las Vegas. Having never attended either event in the past, I knew these two were going to be fun experiences overall due to the "new" factor. Interestingly enough, they both also provided serious moments which grew me into the person I am today.

You see, 2012 was the year in which I began a real fight against anxiety and depression. After a few episodes at the beginning of the year, culminating on my birthday in March with a massive attack, I sought help and began my battle. Coachella Weekend 2 that year was the hottest to date, and if I wasn't trying to forget my problems, I was inside my tent having an attack. Making it through that weekend was difficult, as I was adjusting to the medication while dealing with the heat and other factors…it wasn't easy to say the least. The moment that sticks to my mind from that year was after Dada Life, when everyone decided to bail on the following act Nero except for me. After the few remaining people from my group left for other stages, I found myself alone in a sea of unfamiliar people. It wasn't the best situation, but my desire to see Nero Live pushed me further and further into the crowd until I was as close as possible to the front. Hearing the beautiful live vocals from Alana provided me a moment of serenity, and I lost myself to the music. I gladly gave my soul to Nero, and they gave me back an even deeper love for the beats that moved me.

The follow up just months later in June was EDC Las Vegas 2012. This was EDC's second year in Sin City, and I knew that I needed to attend this event. Let's just talk about Friday though, because that day had the moment which became the reason that I call EDC Las Vegas "home". Upon entering the speedway that year, I never imagined how massive a festival could really be. Coachella sort of hides how big it is with its layout…but this was something else. My excitement levels had already been peaking on the drive out there, and once I was fully in I was just stunned at the amount of people inside. Now I had to navigate a new world, a new chapter of my life, and make some memories along the way. My eyes followed from one end of the speedway to the other, seeing stages, carnival rides, and most importantly people who all probably felt like me. It's a weird type of connection when you feel it for the first time, but if you embrace it you can really feel the energy.

Nothing that year was going to stop me from seeing Above & Beyond, and when the majority of my group bailed to see other acts, it was Todd that stuck with me through the waves of anxiety I faced, over and over. He was nothing but a friend to me as we could feel the energy in the air. Playing probably one of the best sets I'll ever see them play, I was awestruck and completely in love with what Above & Beyond call Group Therapy.

As they hung the breakdown of "Sun & Moon" (you may witness this now during their "push the button" moments), the massive fireworks display drew my attention. It was then when my eyes scanned the crowd around me. People of all backgrounds, sizes, shapes, outfits, were all there together waiting for what was to come. This was before the prevalence of glovers and flow artists so few of these were in the crowd, but it didn't even matter. I was getting pummeled by the lights coming from the stage and the fireworks in the air, it was pure sensory overload. Was this real life? How could this be real? It was like time had stopped, everyone around me had a gigantic smile on their face, and in that moment I realized that I never wanted to leave. Then, the beat dropped and the crowd erupted once again…I knew at that moment I was "home".

I could go on and on, really I could, but those memories are really what shaped me into who I am today as a person. Stories about Burning Man or more recent editions of these same events, adventures with new friends and those who have departed, they're all there still. I have had amazing memories and moments with people since 2012, and I am sure there are more to come. I cannot wait to see what the future holds.

Finally, if I can take anything away from my time here, it is the friend-ships that I have grown over the years. Whether it is my "OG Rave Wife" Patty and the adventures we continue to go on to this day, watching our friend Kevin turn into an amazing glover after years of practice, anytime I've found myself backstage with Angel, or just knowing that no matter what my rave family has my back…this scene has truly provided lifelong friends and memories. Listing out the number of people that have made an impact on my life would be a book in its own, so I hope that everyone understands that I love them dearly and appreciate everything they have offered me. I have so much love for all of you, and I hope that I have been able to provide as much love and happiness to others as well.

Be safe.

28 FEDE FLEITAS - A STATE OF TRANCE ('14)

Fede Fleitas was born and raves in Argentina, and hopes to dance all over the world.

I've been raving in Argentina since 2012. My first love was dubstep and I saw a few shows of it, 'til one of my best friends introduced me to trance music. I used to love dubstep, because I would lose my mind with violent bass lines and higher BPMs, but when I discovered trance, I realized that there was much more. I'm not saying that trance is better than dubstep, techno, hardcore or other genres—in fact, I like almost every single style of electronic music—but with trance, I have a particular relation, because I feel something more with it. In trance music, I find deep feelings, adrenaline, lyrics more beautiful than a sunset in a nice place, and it's always changing. It's very difficult to get bored with a set of pure trance, 'cause you have a moment for every feeling. And if you only wanna dance and jump until the sun rises, trust me, you will.

Well, this feels awkward, because I never talk to anybody about this particular experience. In four years of raving, I've collected a lot of stories that one day I will tell to my sons and grandsons with a big smile on my face, but this particular anecdote talks about one of my happiest moments at a gig:

In 2014, we celebrated "A State Of Trance," Episode 650 in Argentina, and the lineup was integrated by: Ruben De Ronde, Chris Schweizer, Heatbeat, Orjan Nilsen, Dash Berlin, Armin Van Buuren and Aly & Fila. When the day came, I was so excited, because it was my first ASOT experience. But a few hours before the show, I heard that Fadi from Aly & Fila couldn't play, because he had troubles with his passport. So, me and my best friend went to ASOT a little bit sad because we love Fadi and his uplifting trance, but we knew that ASOT would be amazing anyway.

All sets were fantastic. The atmosphere was so kind that I completely forgot the absence of Aly & Fila until the end of Armin Van Buuren's set. Then the final set of the night had come. The organization had added to the lineup a local DJ, Tomas Heredia, for the closing set. He stood up in front of thousands of people waiting for more trance, and opened his set with "Will Atkinson - Watch Out," and everybody became mad.

Then something unimaginable happened: Armin Van Buuren appeared beside him and they started a B2B set. The crowd went crazy, and me and my friend started to walk to the front stage, because we could not believe what we were seeing. When we came to the front, we watched as one by one, all the DJs appeared on the stage and they started to play all together. I was stunned…a B7B set happening right in front of my eyes! I remember every minute from that set. They played a lot of classics and old-school trance like Sandstorm from Darude; Apache and other anthems. That night, I experienced a feeling like none other before. While dancing and jumping, I couldn't stop looking around and all that I saw was a big (BIG) family having a spectacular moment, united by music.

Wherever you put your eyes, a huge smile appeared. Even the DJs were having fun! They was dancing and laughing while playing, and it increased the collective hype.

The B7B set at "A State Of Trance". Dash Berlin, Orjan Nilsen, Chris Schweizer, Tomas Heredia, Armin Van Buuren, Ruben De Ronde and Agustin Servente from Heatbeat. Photo: Fede Fleitas

Then I cried. I really don't know why. Maybe I cried for the uplifting melody that Tomas Heredia was playing, or maybe I cried because I could not believe I was living and dancing...something like that. The fact was that my eyes couldn't hold more tears, and that drove me to dance with even more emotion and passion. It was one of my favorite gigs ever and I will remember it forever.

Also, I appeared dancing in the live stream :)

29 KOSTAS VOULGARIS - MINISTRY OF SOUND ('16)

American/Greek Radio DJ, clubber, trance music columnist (Trancefix.nl), blogger and all around dance music addict.

This is about the first time I got to witness Coldharbour maestro Markus Schulz in action.

Friday the 8th of April 2016, at Ministry Of Sound, London (UK).

I have been a fan of Markus Schulz for years, but I never had the privilege to witness one of his epic sets. I discovered Markus in 2005 when I became pleasantly surprised with his dark, moody signature sound, the sound of "Coldharbour Recordings." Instantly captivated, I became a loyal fan and began collecting his albums and following his radio show, "Global DJ Broadcast," with each year being impressed furthermore by his talent in telling a story with his DJ sets and producing skills. I always knew one day that would come, and as they say, fortune favors the bold. Little did I know that Lady Luck herself was smiling down on me, as I had the honor of witnessing for myself the craft of Markus's Open to Close sets at one of the most iconic clubs in the world--Ministry of Sound, London! What more could one want for his first show??

As tradition has it for a few years now, whenever Markus plays at Ministry the hardcore fans (mostly Schulz Army soldiers) meet for a drink or a bite to eat at the Rockingham Arms Pub beforehand, swapping tales of their clubbing adventures and meeting fellow fans from far and wide. I too had the pleasure of engaging in this tradition, and thus met a nice assortment of people that, like myself, share common ground and pure loyalty to the man himself; people from countries all over the world, who, in fact, display a special devotion to Markus and always make a special effort to see him play wherever he may be. For instance, the people I met included a super-informed and extremely dedicated Belgian, two crazy (in the good sense) brothers from Germany, the Czech Schulz Army team, a mighty cool couple from The Netherlands, and, of course, from the UK. Loyal soldiers of Markus and schooled in all things Coldharbour and its artists, all fueled with a relentless passion and devotion to their leader.

A short walk later, taking in the sights and smells of the night, we arrived at Ministry of Sound. Once inside alongside one of the head honchos of Schulz Army (Fred Leonard), we made our way upstairs to the VIP lounge: an area set with tables, stools and white elegantly dressed couches, including its very own bar and table service. From atop, you could easily catch a glimpse of the crowd partying in the 103 room below, where other DJs were entertaining the crowd with mostly golden classics of dance music. The coolest feature, without a doubt, was beyond the door, where you could get a clear view of the main room (now empty) known as "The Box" which remains closed till 24:00 AM—when the headliner of the night begins his set. From the balcony above, you can catch all the action going on down on the dance floor, as well as hang with fellow dance-music enthusiasts.

The author (R) and DJ/producer Anske in the VIP lounge.
Photo: unknown.

While hanging for a few minutes in the VIP lounge, I was pleasantly surprised to see Markus himself appear walking towards us in his distinct leather jacket. With a broad smile, I greeted him and got to pat him with enthusiasm on the back. Not much time for conversation, unfortunately, as Markus informed us very nicely that he was running late and needed to go set up and prepare the sound check in "The Box." Off he went with the pure dedication of an artist that wants everything to be just right for his audience.

Beaming from the encounter with one of my all-time favorite artists, alongside Fred we entered the artist room backstage, where I was blessed to have had the opportunity to meet and have a small chat with artists such as Adina Butar, Lady V (Victoria Horn) and several others. It was quite special meeting Lady V, as we had conversed on social media for some time but never actually met. The lot found the tale of my journey to London (which consisted of two flights and a lot of waiting in the airports) quite amusing and loaded with dedication as I was flying back out right after the event. A warm and welcoming atmosphere chatting along with them, but it had to be cut short as we moved hastily and eagerly down the stairs and towards the area right next to the DJ booth. This is where I had the rare honor to witness for myself most of the sound check of "The Box" by Markus, who was in high spirits and eager to get things rolling.

Usually you can tell from the very beginning what the general vibe of the night is going to be like and it felt it was going to be a journey like no other. This was indeed the case and then some.

Slowly but steadily, the fury of the dark, moody, enthralling sound that we Schulz fans all love was unleashed by the maestro of Coldharbour himself. Many favorites that have become staples in his sets were present, such as "M.I.K.E. Push vs. Rank1-Zenith," "Arkham Knights-Knightfall" and "Legacy" and even fantastic mashups such as "Dies Radion6 vs. Markus Schulz & Vassy – Tomorrow Never from Salvation (Markus Schulz Mashup)," and "Cosmic Gate vs. Dash Berlin & Andrew Rayel vs. Adina Butar – Leave My Body Till the am2pm Falls Down (Markus Schulz Mashup)."

New material was premiered as well, as he teased us by showcasing tracks from his new artist album such as "A Better You" and the new stalker anthem entitled "In the Night (featuring Brooke Tomlinson)," which sent chills down our spine as we gleefully danced, shouting the main chorus. A highlight of this unveiling of gems from his box of delights was Lady V joining him in the booth, full of love for her craft, dancing and entertaining the audience alongside Markus while her collaboration with him, "Watch The World," stormed the crowd—her distinct, entrancing voice soaring and captivating our minds as we watched the world from high above. Watching the crowd dancing frantically from my bird's-eye view, I was in awe of the electrifying atmosphere crafted elegantly by Markus, as well as the magical light show consisting of visuals on the screen behind the booth and lasers of many colors that stormed the floor below. Among fellow Schulz Army members from The Netherlands, Belgium, The UK and beyond we all danced with wide smiles carved on our faces, all connected and united by our love and admiration for the artist and sound that we love.

Relentless, and with an energy that few attain, he pushed forward, delivering serious punishment to the dance floor with passion and desire to see a smile on everyone's faces, hands in the air firing away with one bomb after another, while the smoke cannons engulfed the box with a refreshing mist, smiling all the way.

Other artists were there as well, such as Anske (Andrej Anskinas), Danny Cullen (Artisan), Marcus White, Dennis Sheperd and Adina Butar, cheering and showing their support for the captain of the Coldharbour ship. Chatting often with Anske through social media as well as Danny Cullen (from his Tucandeo alias days) and Marcus White, it was fantastic to finally get to meet them all in person, have a small chat amidst the dancing and even grab their autographs, which they so graciously gave. It was a rare honor to meet and party alongside them, I must tell you. Another cool moment was definitely chatting a bit with Lady V about her music and taking pictures together while she was in the booth with Markus. Such pleasant people to be around, so radiant and full of life and passion for their art. Certainly gaining my respect and valuing them even more as individuals, as well as the talented artists that they are.

The evident love for dance music connected people from far and wide, spreading high-energy vibes all across the dance floor as everyone lifted their hands high in the air in utter admiration and appreciation for the mystical voyage Markus was taking us all on.

Eventually, there came a moment in the night when things took a darker, twisted turn down empty corridors and barren wastelands of far-away lands. Markus took hold of the microphone, warning us that we

Markus Schulz, in "The Box." Photo: Kostas Voulgaris

had arrived at his favorite part of the night, a time when things get a little strange and weird. That was without a doubt the infamous "Rabbit Hole" phenomenon.

I must say I was eager to tumble head first down the Rabbit Hole myself and discover the darkest, techier part of the night, letting the darkness consume me while the lights, visuals and strobes played leading roles in the experience: Techy, stripped-down rhythms emphasizing the drums and beat, while eerie voices bellowed through the speakers as the crowd danced, almost hypnotically entranced by the sounds Markus bestowed upon them. There is no greater joy, I believe, than to witness the artist (in this case, Markus) enjoying himself just as much as the enthralled audience, as he grinned widely from ear to ear dancing accordingly and moving his hands to the beat. We cast our worries or whatever problems we may have in our life aside with ease while emotions of inner bliss overcame us. Everyone dancing with the sincerest of smiles on our faces, our senses tingling from the high of the music.

Legend has it that once one emerges from the Rabbit Hole, they find themselves changed, becoming a better version of themselves. That was absolutely true this night as we came out of the Hole charged with radiance, a mass amount of positive vibes within and our endorphins were rushing like a racehorse on the track.

Other grand moments were when his own vocal tracks such as "Destiny (featuring Delacey)" and "Facedown (featuring Soundlab)" were dropped. The audience sang along with joy and vigor, completely living through the lyrics and beat of the music, offering their respect towards the man himself.

Mayhem was being unleashed by Markus and the audience all over "The Box," as well as us were all loving it! At that point, with a heavy heart I realized the time had come to sadly leave the event and my new friends. It was 4:30 am and I must say I could easily go on for hours more but, unfortunately, I had to catch my bus to the airport as I had an early flight out of London. I embraced and bid goodbye to my new friends one by one, thanking them for the experience and wishing them all the best, hoping to see them all again in the near-future.

It is evident some people are destined to follow specific paths in their lives. Markus is doing exactly what he was meant to do, giving us goose-bumps with his divine performances and flooding the world with dark gems from the depths of his lively imagination, and Coldharbour itself.

A night I would certainly describe as legendary, and I am happy to have had the privilege to witness it for myself!

Till next time, I will treasure all the memories from this divine night in London!

Photo: Kostas Voulgaris

30 CAITLYN CORAPI - PARENTS WHO PLUR ('14)

Caitlyn Corapi is a young electronic music journalist.

The bass is pounding through the speakers, pulsing up my legs and beating through my chest. Lasers stretch across the sky in the shape of long triangles, pinching in and out and flashing different colors. The inside of the massive tent stage is pitch black, with flashes of light illuminating the faces around me in varying shades: blue, pink, white, and the green hue from the lasers. I turn to look at Thumper and Pussycat, who are locked in a loving embrace, whispering (or yelling over the music) to each other. Thumper is dressed in his homemade King Tut-inspired costume. It's a mask of a deer skull—an emblem of his and his wife's favorite DJ, Porter Robinson, which he had painted a goldish-bronze color and laced with glowing light rope earlier that day while still awake from the night before. Pussycat had prepared a deer costume (it's her spirit animal) with a similar, more feminine mask, but has chosen to wear comfort over costume—a pink T-shirt and Capri pants with sneakers. With thousands of people surrounding them, they act as if they are the only ones in the world. I look up at the stage for a second and turn back to find them kissing passionately.

Not the kind of kiss where you think, "Gross, get a room," but the kind that makes you think, "Holy shit, they are so in love."

It's hard to stick with them through Electric Daisy Carnival in Orlando as they wander between stages and through crowds, hands clasped tight. They frequently get on various rides, their favorite being the Ferris Wheel—and through all the controlled chaos, they never leave each other's sight. They spend two days blissed out and dancing, and let the stress of their normal lives melt away. Man, I've never seen real adults in such pure bliss (since, you know, being a twenty-something isn't really adulthood).

Electric Daisy Carnival is a festival put together by the longtime famous promoter, Pasquale Rotella and his company, Insomniac. He's been throwing raves (parties involving dancing, drinking, and general madness) since the 1990s, when he started out underground in Southern California warehouses. This was what would give birth to the original EDC. It took years for it to become what is it today—twenty, in fact—as EDC Las Vegas just celebrated its twentieth birthday last June. It was the biggest event yet in its history, and something like 400,000+ people attended over the course of the three days it was held.

The festival had been forced out of California in part because of headlines in the media that focused almost totally on the drug use at raves, and this continues to be an issue for ravers in what was once the rave capital of the United States. In contrast, Las Vegas welcomed EDC with open arms in 2011. Since its debut there, EDC has grossed over $1 billion for the local economy, as well as increased the number of visitors to Las Vegas by 1.7 million, while creating thousands of full-time jobs. The same year EDC made its move to Las Vegas, they also began their venture in

Orlando. Today, EDC has done events in Chicago, New York, London, Mexico, India and more.

Prior to walking through the gates on the second and final day of their festivities, Pussycat and Thumper toasted their MDMA caps and Jell-O shots, before chasing one with the other. MDMA, also known as Molly or Ecstasy, is a drug sometimes used at these events, though it is not unique to the rave scene. The effects of the drug are euphoria, increased sensations of positive feelings and emotions, and increased heart rate (also profuse sweating—which no one seems to mind here). This is what is referred to as rolling. Insomniac is aware of its popularity, and they state clearly in all of their promotions that they do not tolerate its use at their events. Onsite, there are six foot-tall signs outside of each bathroom area that say: "MDMA ALERT: Extremely dangerous MDMA (aka Molly/Ecstasy) is becoming increasingly common. While drug use is extremely prohibited at this event, there is a chance people will, against these rules, illegally sneak drugs into this venue." There are accompanying bullet points and a website listed as well that encourage people to say something if they see something, and security is everywhere.

When Thumper and Pussycat engage in the recreational use of MDMA, which they've informed me is only strictly at these kinds of events once or twice a year, they start to act like a couple who've just gotten together—completely obsessed with everything about the other. I usually refer to this as the honeymoon stage, and it's intriguing to see it with a couple who have been together for almost nine years.

Pussycat is 44 years old and has lived a very interesting life, to say the least. She is a non-practicing psychotherapist who spent many years working in a maximum-security prison (today she just focuses on being a mom). During this period of her life, she was married to a narcotics officer. "There's no other way to say it, I was a bitch. I was not the nonjudgmental, open person that I am now. It took a lot of me growing up and realizing who I was."

She explains that her younger brother was always the "black sheep" of the family growing up, and that he was into raves, which bothered her. "I just didn't understand the lifestyle. I was a pretentious cunt and told him to get away from the people he was associating with and get rid of this weird lifestyle. I told him to be like normal people. I had no idea it had nothing to do with how you dress or what time you went to bed." Pussycat and her ex-husband were firm believers in the simplistic idea of electronic music directly correlating to drug abuse. As in, "All of the bad stuff coming from the raves were the drugs, and the music made you want to do the drugs."

She grew up in a heavily wooded area in northern Michigan, with an alcoholic, abusive father. "I was trailer trash," she says today. "Whenever my dad would abuse me, I would run out of the back of the trailer and hide in the woods. I would sit under trees and the deer would never run from me." She lights up a cigarette (when home, she doesn't allow her seven-year-old son on the porch when she is smoking) and tells me more about her brother, confessing that she had the wrong impressions of everything he was into, and didn't realize until she was older that his deep-rooted "black sheep" issues had more to do with his upbringing than the scene he was involved in.

She had compared electronic music shows to hip-hop shows: "I went to college near Detroit, and hip-hop [there] was nasty. I would walk into a club when I was 19 and people were fighting, everyone had guns—I wouldn't dare walk into the club and touch someone by accident." She can't recall a time she has ever felt that unsafe at a rave.

Thumper and Pussycat were both married to other people when they met. They became infatuated with each other and spent months having an affair. Thumper recalls "driving three and half hours every weekend just to see her," when they were both living in Florida. Becoming parents together was the biggest surprise for them, when Pussycat found herself pregnant, even though her tubes were tied. "It was a major shock," Thumper remembers, "New life came out of nowhere and completely changed my life for the better. I knew I always wanted to be a good father, because I didn't get that from my parents."

Thumper, 37, grew up on the West Coast. He attended middle school and high school in California, but spent most of his life in Washington state. "My dad was a free roaming hippie; I didn't see him at all in my years in California." He explains how his father had followed a religious Hindu cult, so when Thumper was little, his dad would take him to temples across the U.S. and even in other countries. Following a long separation, Thumper went back to visit his father in his new home in New Orleans in 1999. "He said he'd found this thing and it was something all of the hippies in the '60s and '70s were looking for but didn't have. He said it was a rave and he said the music was good, the people were good, and the drugs were great," he laughs as he says this.

Thumper's first rave in NOLA was a mesmerizing experience for him. "I was blown away by the laser lights and pounding music and tons of people everywhere. People were in big groups and they were really friendly."

Many were wearing neon colors, fluffy socks, tutus, and kandi bracelets. A kandi bracelet is made of plastic beads, usually called pony beads in stores, and ravers often spend hundreds of hours and dollars making these bracelets to give away and trade at events.

Pussycat had made me a bracelet with my newly appointed "rave name," and now she puts her hand up to mine and forms a Peace sign, motioning for me to do the same. Our index and middle fingers touch and then she curves her fingers into a half heart. I follow and do the same so that our hands together form a full heart, symbolic of Love. Her hand goes flat and she pushes my hand flat against hers: Unity. We spread our fingers and lock them together: Respect. That's the rave mantra: PLUR. Peace, Love, Unity, Respect.

While our hands are still locked together, she slides a bracelet off her wrist and onto mine. It reads "SHARKFIN" in letter blocks, surrounded by a pattern of colors and a whistle. She even surprises me with a pink shark onesie that is extremely cozy and exceptionally cute. She does this again with another bracelet, this one reads "SWEETUMS," and has a daisy charm on it. This is the name she calls me all the time now, even when we aren't at a rave.

Thumper admits to taking pressed ecstasy pills at the NOLA rave, the kind that look like Sweet Tarts candy. "There was a Mitsubishi stamp on them. You know how they say your first roll is always your hardest? That was definitely true for me." His dad had supplied the pills, but when Thumper really started feeling them, he decided to wander off on his own and explore the scene. He discovered that there were multiple rooms that were all decorated completely differently, playing all different styles of music. He found his way to a room playing drum and bass, which would become his favorite style of electronic music, and he was amazed at the graffiti on the walls glowing in the black light. "I was an artist at the time and graffiti was kind of my thing."

The most interesting thing about this experience for Thumper was the environment. "I had been to New Orleans a few times for Mardi Gras and it left a bad taste in my mouth, because it never felt safe or comfortable, but when I went to the rave, I felt different, safe—everyone was really friendly." This was when Thumper first discovered PLUR.

Pussycat didn't attend her first festival until EDC Orlando 2014. Thumper had gone in 2013 with her brother and had had an amazing, life-changing experience, and insisted that she come with him the next year. He says this event turned things around for him, since the year leading up to then had been one of the toughest in his life. He had almost lost Pussycat due to illness and multiple surgeries she had undergone, while someone at his job whom he'd considered close had screwed him over badly (which had devastated him), and he says he had made a lot of stupid decisions to add to all of it.

When he walked through the gates and saw how professionally put together EDC was, he was shocked. He had been established professionally in the IT field, climbing the ladder for success for some time by that point, but hadn't understood until then how much energy and dedication could be put into festivals. He realized then that this wasn't just about people going out and partying: for some people, this was their career, and they took pride in their work. For both of them, the first EDC experiences were spent sober; they were both awakened by the music alone. Pussycat tells me, "I was born in 1972 and awakened in 2014. I did not feel fully alive till then. The people, the music, the PLUR—that's a feeling that no drug can give you."

She has felt that her past had left her jaded, judgmental, and pretentious, and that her first festival experience in 2014 changed all of that. She left feeling like an addict chasing a high for the music and for PLUR: She'd "melted into the music in the dusty, humid air." This year at EDC Orlando, she had a very similar experience: "I felt like I had let 20 years of stress and pretentiousness completely sweat and dissolve off me, and it started raining and it cleansed me. It was my second spiritual awakening. I stood in front of two laser owls in the rain and had an awakening."

Now, they bob and weave through the massive crowds together at EDC in 2016, stopping to talk to people and dance, and, of course, kiss each other. They are always side-by-side or holding hands. We move between three massive stages freely. The tent stage from earlier is the Neon Garden, which houses the trance and techno DJs. Circuit Grounds is the second largest, with massive rectangle-shaped LED screens that surround the crowd, the biggest being in the center, flanked by smaller ones on both sides, diminishing in size the further they spread out. This stage is home to the heavy bass music for the weekend, like dubstep. One of the most popular DJs in the scene, Bassnectar, will perform on this stage second to last tonight, followed by the West Coast legend, RL Grime.

The third stage, which is the biggest and most famous, is the Kinetic Field, where Thumper and Pussycat had watched the Porter Robinson set earlier that night. A circular screen of LEDs is centered between two giant columns on each side, each column sporting two enormous owls that stare out over the crowd. As impressive as this is, all three of these stages are actually smaller renditions of the ones that are put together for EDC Las Vegas, meaning the ones in Vegas can be three to four times the size. I can't even imagine what that would be like, since the two big stages here are probably six stories high.

People nearby are always turning to dance with us or try to shove blunts in our faces, which we respectfully decline, and with good reason. Pussycat had a bad experience a few months prior, when they'd met up with someone at a Porter Robinson show, who they had first met at an earlier festival. Pussycat had taken a hit from a blunt that was not actually weed and found herself vomiting and paranoid that Thumper was plotting to kill her. "We have gotten to a point where we don't need to take things from other people. We get our own, and while we can share, it's not the worth the risk of not knowing if someone is telling you what they really have. I told my daughter about this experience and it stuck with her. I don't think she'll ever make that mistake. On the car ride down here, we were on the phone and she said, 'Don't smoke anyone's weed, mom!'" Her daughter is in her twenties and lives on the West Coast, with a family of her own. This makes me consider that a bad experience happening to a stranger makes kids think "it won't happen to me," but when it's someone like a parent telling you it *did* happen to them, it's bound to hit the kid harder.

EDM music genres range from house music (and its many sub-genres), to dubstep, techno, trance, disco, drum and bass, and so much more. Its vast, growing popularity has made many artists not from the EDM world hop on the train—like world-famous guitarist, Tom Morello, who is featured in a song by Knife Party (a dubstep/electro-house/drum and bass

DJ). Even Coldplay has been featured by many DJs remixing a lot of their songs.

There are a lot of common misconceptions and negative stigmas regarding the music, and I know firsthand, because I was once one of those people who ragged on it. Everyone thinks EDM is "that techno shit, right?" Everybody seems to hate techno for some reason and Pussycat admitted to hating it because of that lyric in an Eminem song, "Nobody listens to techno!" The crazy part is, just about everyone has at some point listened to electronic music, and maybe, in fact, enjoyed it without realizing it.

You've probably heard one of Calvin Harris' anthems, such as "Feel So Close," "Summer," and "This is What You Came For," featuring Rihanna on vocals. Harris is an electrohouse/electropop DJ, and admittedly he has some extremely catchy songs. Then there's Major Lazer, an EDM group featuring Diplo, Jillionaire and Walshy Fire, that has Jamaican beats and some Brazilian inspired drum lines. One of their most recent famous hits called "Lean On" could be heard anywhere, from the radio to the grocery store. Diplo also teamed up with another extremely popular artist, Skrillex, to create a group called Jack U—most famous for their hit song with Justin Bieber entitled "Where Are U Now". There's a Coca-Cola commercial featuring a song titled "Candyman" by a DJ named Zedd, and all of the anti-smoking and Mountain Dew Kickstart commercials feature songs from DJs growing in popularity every month. And then there's The Chainsmokers, who have blown up in the past year. They received a lot of recognition following the release of "Roses" and a summer smash hit, "Don't Let Me Down," and most recently, "Closer," which have all been overplayed on the radio and pretty much any store you go to.

This is the third festival that I've attended myself, and I must say it is by the far the best. As I look around, I see happiness on everyone's faces and it's really difficult to find someone that isn't having fun. New friendships are being built, strangers are becoming family, and I even witness young girls twerking on an old man selling water bottles in the crowd. I laugh when I see this, as the old, heavyset man with white hair has a bucket of ice filled with drinks on his head, a big open-mouth smile and a bright red face. "How else is he supposed to react to that?" I muse.

I had heard someone on the radio a few days before the festival saying, "Whoever said Disney was the most magical place on earth has never been to EDC." After witnessing what I've seen this weekend and feeling the overall vibes of the festival itself, it's a statement that Thumper, Pussycat and I can get behind. Thumper tells me the ideal family vacation would be taking your kids to Disney for a few days and then leaving them with grandma so mom and dad can go to EDC and experience some magic, too.

We pick a spot to sit on: a small bench attached to a massive glowing daisy, so I can ask them about their rave names. Even being far from all three stages, the ground rumbles and the sound of the music pulses around us. Pussycat has two rave names, her second one being Rave Mom. "People I met would start calling me Festival Mom, because I would stop and talk to young girls who looked like they were in trouble. I would ask them if they wanted to go get some water or where their friends were, where their phone was, stuff like that. Pussycat I got from Thumper. I have always been a controlling, type-A personality, organized and in line. At our first festival together, EDC Orlando 2014, he kept saying 'Relax,

Pussycat! It's a new way of life!' So that one is really personal."

Thumper got his nickname in a personal way as well, but that story was much dirtier. "She told me I fuck like a rabbit after raves," his smile reaches from ear to ear. His obvious pride is showing.

We watch as people walk by in carnival attire on stilts, with faces full of makeup and puffy black wigs. They laugh and dance as they walk, stopping to take pictures with other festivalgoers. There is a man whose entire body is painted to look like a green lizard, with giant white paper spikes attached to his head, and a tiny piece of black cloth covering his parts. The body paint has all types of shades and lines that morph his body into something otherworldly looking. There is another man dressed casually in a T-shirt and shorts, with a neon green wig on that goes down to the middle of his back. Some girls are dressed in "booty shorts," which are just sparky thongs with different cutout shapes on the sides, and pasties (stickers shaped like aliens, peace signs, or xs) just barely covering their nipples. Others are dressed in long, flowy skirts or one-piece bathing suits, and some are even dressed in full animal costumes.

There is definitely a large celebration of expression radiating through the masses of people—no one is self-conscious, everyone is comfortable. "I like that people can wear so little and it not be a sexual thing," Thumper says. At least, that is how he feels; I'm sure there are others who would disagree. He also notes that when you go to a regular carnival, the people working there look miserable and strung out. "Here, the person you buy your food from is going to be dancing next to you on day two," he says as he removes his deer mask, revealing beads of sweat dripping from his short hair down his forehead. His smile is big and he's always flashing it. It's rare to see him without it pasted across his face. Pussycat looks at him lovingly while he talks, sweat trickling down from her shoulder-length, light blonde hair.

Later that night, we sit down together poolside at the house we're renting off-site. They are still amped and looking for an after-party; there is an overwhelming sense of *this can't be over already*. This has been a weekend we had anticipated for months and it definitely did not disappoint. We've partied for two glorious days "under the electric sky" (as it's often referred to), and made friendships that will last forever. We toast to an amazing festival with Jell-O shots, with Pussycat adding her special touch by putting them in large, penis-shaped syringes. She had started off my weekend by shoving one in my mouth and forcing me to take it, and we laugh now about the pictures that Thumper had taken while this went on.

I ask about their son, Reed, who is seven and autistic, and completely obsessed with electronic music already. I can honestly admit he knows more DJs than I do. Pussycat tells me that Reed had taught his best friend about kandi trading and PLUR. "This is something he knows: what is peace, what is love, what is respect? These are our commandments. We respect people for who they are, and these are values that we're putting into our child."

Reed was taken to his first show on Pussycat's 44th birthday this year. They went as a family to see Deadmau5, "And we were stone-cold sober," she says. "We didn't even drink a beer. We're very different when we're mom and dad." They tell me that the Deadmau5 show was one of the only places they felt comfortable letting Reed go up to strangers and interact with them. "People kept coming up to him, dancing with him and talking to him, teaching him hooping and poi. You can't go to a park and let your son walk up to a stranger, but you can at a music festival." Pussycat starts to tear up when recalling the show with their son, mentioning that Reed had pulled her up to the silent disco stage, where they danced together. "We had done that stuff in the living room, but never in front of so many people."

They are both excited about bringing their son to more shows and festivals as he gets older. "He got upset because he couldn't go to EDC, so I told him I would take him at 16 to his first EDC," Thumper says, Pussycat pointing out that Reed would have to be 18 to go. "I don't think, as a parent, I'll ever be ready for my son to go and be independent, because I'm so close to him," he continues. "It terrifies me for him to go out into the world, but I know when he's ready, I'll be able to handle it. I would love to experience those things with him when he's old enough, but still young enough to enjoy it with me. I want to show him all of the options and things that he can do and achieve. It could be that he goes and sees the carnival rides and wants to build them and become an engineer." Pussycat had told me earlier that Reed has a fascination with how things work, so it wouldn't be too surprising to me if he did end up creating and building things eventually.

I ask them a question that I figure no parent would readily have an answer for: "What about the drugs? Are you afraid that he'll grow up and do them? Are you going to ever find yourself having the don't do drugs conversation?" They admit that they haven't had the conversation yet and don't exactly anticipate having it—at least, not in the traditional sense. "This is his first year in DARE and we chuckle at the information packets he brings home, but our approach will be different," Pussycat says. "We hope to catch it before he ever does experiment. We want him to know before he does it that we have both done it and how to do it safely and test things. We will never buy his drugs, but we will buy test kits. Just like when he's old enough to have a girlfriend and start having sex, we'll buy him condoms."

She stays calm and collected through this conversation. "Drugs are everywhere; he can find them at the playground. It's important that he's smart about it and knows what he's doing for the safety of all of us." From my perspective, I also think it's pretty reasonable to say that telling a kid not to do something isn't always the best method, seeing as a majority of parents use this method and kids still grow up to experiment. This isn't a conversation singled out for parents who listen to electronic music either, for every type of music or concert has some vice associated with it. People get hammered at many different types of shows, which Pussycat confirms, while laughing: "One of the drunkest I've ever been was at a jazz festival drinking wine. Like, I literally had to be carried out!"

The scene is growing larger, and as raves become more commonplace and more people start to get involved, it doesn't seem so underground anymore. There's no doubt that new generations coming up are more accepting of these massive parties full of flashing, glowing, colorful lights that people from all walks of life and ages are attending. Pussycat admits it's the older generations, like her friends, that only view it with negative stigmas. "My friends that I've had for years and years are shocked that I'm into this, but then I show them pictures and they tell me it actually looks really fun," she says as we make our way from the backyard to their Subaru

Outback. "Older people aren't seeing EDM festivals as they are, they're seeing them how they first came up." The importance of electronic dance music becoming more mainstream is the fact that a lot of the negative aspects can be avoided and myths can be busted.

While there are a large number of college kids attending the festival, there are also upstanding members of the workforce letting loose, too. The day before, I had met a man with hundreds of pieces of kandi jewelry, all with elaborate perlers attached (I used to love making perlers when I was a child, and was excited to see that they're so popular in the scene). He was an attractive man in his mid to late '30s and looked like he worked out a lot, dressed in a gladiator costume with a giant helmet made completely of pony beads and a staff, which held most of his perlers. "I'm an accountant, I just get bored and make these," he told me.

When I ask Pussycat if she thinks the scene will become safer, she responds, "Absolutely. More people are now talking about good experiences and bad experiences and I think they're making more informed decisions." The more people talk about things like bad trips, people not staying hydrated, bad batches of Molly going around—the safer it is for everyone. People are more informed. "Let's not call it drug abuse, let's call it drug education, drug information."

While they both enjoy the rave scene and meeting new people, Pussycat has admitted that she has always led a very guarded life and makes sure that their home life is protected and safe. They usually end up together after a show in a hotel room or partying in someone else's room, but they never bring someone they just met into their home environment. "In a professional world, I would lose credibility if I told them that a few times a year, I party with strangers, dance with strangers, do drugs, and even have ended up naked with strangers! Other than that, I am the soccer mom and the wife who does the dry cleaning and stands next to her husband at an event in fancy clothes. We are functional members of society that occasionally go and let loose!" Her husband is now an IT bank executive, and their daily life outside of festivals is very normal compared to other people their ages. "Except grocery shopping," she chuckles, "I will always hate grocery shopping!"

It takes longer than expected to round up the party crew in the house, get them in the car and on the road for the after-party (close to 3:00 AM). I ask Pussycat one more thing, "Why the deer costumes?" She tells me that deer are her spirit animals and that they chose her. She recalls when they wouldn't run from her as a child after being beaten. She tells me when her daughter was five, she had been kicked by a colt in the backwoods of Michigan. Knowing an ambulance couldn't get back to them, she frantically tried to drive to the hospital. "The skin wasn't broken, but I knew it was bad," she says. "As I was driving out of the woods, a deer jumped in front of the car and there was no way around it. I turned back to my screaming daughter to find the skin had broken on the wound. I ripped my shirt off and tied it around her to compress it." She was later told by the doctor at the hospital that if she had not done that, her daughter would have bled out.

She also tells me that while she and Thumper were having their affair, they would see deer everywhere they went. "We were at the Hilton in D.C. and looked out the window and saw deer—in the middle of the city," she laughs. She remembers an earlier time canoeing at the Suwannee Lake in

Florida when they first started meeting up, when they'd wound up on protected land: "We were in that stage where we would have sex any chance
we could, so we did right there in the wild, and when we finished, a fawn
walked right up to us and laid down alongside us." She said, "Immediately
after, my father had called me and told me he didn't think my [sick] grandmother was going to make it—I rushed home to see her and she passed
the next morning." She claims that deer have always been there to comfort
or warn her of something, hence her sons name being "deer" backwards.

The clock is about to strike 3:00 and we're on the road, but then it goes
back to 2:00. We cheer, an extra hour in the club—thank you, Daylight Sav-
ing Time! Another friend tells a story about Reed, how he had downloaded
the Santa app and was using it to prank call Santa. Pussycat and Thumper
laugh. "He's a trip," she says. I can see the reflection of Thumper's face in
the window, the same face he makes anytime someone mentions his son:
a true look of happiness, bliss, kind of like the one I had seen on both of
their faces earlier at the festival. I thought of what Thumper had told me
a few days prior: "Having a child doesn't mean you have to stop being human and having fun."

A month later I am sitting in Pussycat and Thumper's living room on
their brown microfiber sectional, covered in all of Reed's blankets and toys.
What had started with just a few of his favorite stuffed animals around my
head has turned into an unloading of the contents of his room, which are
now smothering me. I can hear his muffled giggles as he jumps on top of
me, searching for a hole to stick a feather through and tickle my face with.
Pussycat and Thumper sit at their kitchen table, sipping mugs of coffee

and scrolling through social media. The fireplace is roaring, making the house warm up on this cold rainy day. Deer decorate the mantle and the canvasses above it.

"Oh my gosh!" I hear Thumper say. I flop everything off of me and peek my head out.

"What?" I say.

"There was a warehouse fire in Oakland, nine dead and twenty-five missing."

I jump up in shock and run to the table. Peering over his shoulder, I see the article title: *"Ghost Ship Fire, Warehouse Rave May Have Killed 30."* For the rest of the day, we continue to refresh our browsers and Google updates. Most of the people in the fire were young kids or middle-aged, and one of the people who lost their life was a visualizer for some of the most famous DJs out right now. The news baffles us and we are heartbroken.

"That could have been me," Thumper says, "I would have totally gone to an event like that."

It could have been any of us. It could have been anyone we met at EDC or some other festival. It's probable that someone we made a connection with at an event has family or friends that were there. That's why our hearts ache for our fellow rave family. It's not just about getting messed up and partying, it's about the connections you make and the family you build. It's watching out for each other, being there for each other—even after the event.

Underground raves are becoming increasingly obsolete now that many nightclubs, parks, and racetracks are willing to rent their space out for events like this. However, they are not totally gone. Often people consider these raves to be the "true" scene, because they aren't mainstream. However, a lot of these places don't have permits, aren't regulated, and lack proper inspections, which can make them dangerous. While it may be fun to be able to see DJs no one knows about yet or have a hot night out in a house-party type environment, to me it isn't worth it for the risks. The growing popularity of these parties means people like me want to see more like EDC, safe and professional, and less like Ghost Ship. Thumper and Pussycat know, though, that when Reed is ready to rave, he'll be going to EDC.

GLOSSARY OF TERMS

Acid House – A form of Chicago house music at the center of the birth and massive expansion of the original UK rave scene in the late 1980s.

Acid Line - A popular element of many dance songs, noted for use of repetitive notation, and employing a filter that has a moving cutoff point.

BPM – Beats Per Minute, on a dance track.

Burners – Regular attendees of the "Burning Man" festival.

Club Kids – A sub-genre of electronic music fans who dress in highly provocative androgynous and/or gender bending fashion, makeup and the like. First observed in NYC in the early 1990s.

Criminal Justice Act – A 1994 British law designed in part to target raves and shut them down, viewed by many in the electronic music community as draconian in nature.

Cubase – A music software product developed by German musical software company Steinberg for music recording, arranging and editing.

Decks – DJ tables; can be vinyl turntables or CD players.

DIY – Do It Yourself, an ethos central to the original rave scene, as well as the early punk and hip-hop scenes.

Double stacks – Twice the usual dosage of MDMA.

EDC – Electric Daisy Carnival, a massive electronic music festival and tour produced by Insomniac Productions.

EDM – Electronic Dance Music.

Fire poi – Fiery, whirling performance art involving a pair of arm-length chains with handles attached to one end, and a bundle of flammable wicking material on the other.

Flyer – Paper promotional items used to advertise parties, much like rock posters in the 1960s, except smaller. Usually containing an address or telephone info lines for directions.

Gloving - White or black gloves with an LED light at the end of each fingertip. A glover will move their hands around to create trails of light for the person(s) receiving a show. The movements are often incorporated to the beat of the music.

Glow sticks – Chemically-powered light sticks used by ravers to create trail effects similar to gloving, used mostly prior to the invention of LED fashion.

House – House music. The original mid-1980s music born in Chicago warehouses that eventually changed the dance music world, which now has too many sub-genres to mention here.

Insomniac – An electronic music event production company founded by rave promoter Pasquale Rotella.

Kandi (or Candy) – A form of rave fashion, its main elements being colorful beads, bracelets, necklaces, hats, boots and more.

Map point – A scavenger hunt-like system used to direct ravers to a secret party location. Also refers to the spot where ravers pick up maps to the party itself.

Massive – An old rave term for a very large party, usually upwards of 5,000 people.

MDMA – 3,4-methylenedioxy-methamphetamine, a.k.a. Ecstasy. A popular rave party drug. Also known as E, X, Batmans, Mitsubishis, and other names.

MIDI - Musical Instrument Digital Interface: a protocol developed in the 1980's which allows electronic instruments and other digital musical tools to communicate with each other.

Molly – A more recent Ecstasy-like drug which usually contains very little MDMA, and is "cut" with other often illegal substances.

Perlers – A bunch of small plastic perler beads melted together by an iron to create pictures. Used in raving fashion, like kandi.

PLUR – Peace, Love, Unity, Respect – rave mantra coined by DJ Frankie Bones.

Rolling – Feeling the euphoric effects of MDMA.

Tripping balls – Being under the influence of psychedelics.

Twerking – Highly suggestive dancing by female partygoers, made particularly famous by Miley Cyrus. A very late addition to the rave scene.

Warehouse party – exactly what it sounds like.

WMC – Winter Music Conference, an annual electronic music industry gathering in Miami that takes place every March.

ABOUT THE EDITOR

MICHAEL TULLBERG is one of the longest-running and most respected electronic music photojournalists in North America. Beginning in 1996, Michael comprehensively covered the rave scene across the country, and around the world as well. Through the peak years of the rave scene in the 1990s and 2000s, Michael's images, interviews and articles appeared in the pages of magazines such as Rolling Stone, SPIN, URB, BPM Culture, Mixer, Insider, Mixmag, Q, Hybrid (Japan), Lotus, and others—more than any other electronic music photojournalist of the period. During that era, he also shot album covers for several of the world's major dance music DJs and artists, including icons like Carl Cox, Ferry Corsten and DJ Dan.

Michael is the author of DANCEFLOOR THUNDERSTORM: Land of The Free, Home Of The Rave, the groundbreaking coffee table photo book about the rise of electronic music in North America. The first book of its kind in the U.S., DANCEFLOOR THUNDERSTORM contains hundreds of vintage photographs, DJ interviews, rave fliers and memorabilia. It has won praises from the likes of Mixmag, VICE, Buzzfeed, Insomniac. com, Paper, and more.

Today, Michael photographs for Getty Images, contributing entertainment pictures from the red carpet, concerts and celebrity benefits. He is also the CEO of 5150 Publishing, an independent book publishing house established to put out works devoted to electronic music, and pop culture in general. He contributes a monthly column to DJ Mag. And, he still shoots raves when he can find the time.

CPSIA information can be obtained
at www.ICGtesting.com
Printed in the USA
FSOW04n0706140817
37578FS